Manifesting

A Method for Manifesting Exceptional Wealth

(How to Master and Apply Abundance Mindset in Your Life)

Myrtle Thurman

Published By **Jackson Denver**

Myrtle Thurman

All Rights Reserved

Manifesting: A Method for Manifesting Exceptional Wealth (How to Master and Apply Abundance Mindset in Your Life)

ISBN 978-1-77485-592-8

No part of this guidebook shall be reproduced in any form without permission in writing from the publisher except in the case of brief quotations embodied in critical articles or reviews.

Legal & Disclaimer

The information contained in this ebook is not designed to replace or take the place of any form of medicine or professional medical advice. The information in this ebook has been provided for educational & entertainment purposes only.

The information contained in this book has been compiled from sources deemed reliable, and it is accurate to the best of the Author's knowledge; however, the Author cannot guarantee its accuracy and validity and cannot be held liable for any errors or omissions. Changes are periodically made to this book. You must consult your doctor or get professional medical advice before using any of the suggested remedies, techniques, or information in this book.

Upon using the information contained in this book, you agree to hold harmless the Author from and against any damages, costs, and expenses, including any legal fees potentially resulting from the application of any of the information provided by this guide. This disclaimer applies to any damages or injury caused by the use and application, whether directly or indirectly, of any advice or information presented, whether for breach of contract, tort, negligence, personal injury, criminal intent, or under any other cause of action.

You agree to accept all risks of using the information presented inside this book. You need to consult a professional medical practitioner in order to ensure you are both able and healthy enough to participate in this program.

Table of Contents

Chapter 1: Why It Hasn't Worked For Me Yet 1

Chapter 2: Why Manifestation Didn't Work Out For You 10

Chapter 3: Building A Strong Oneness 19

Chapter 4: How To Visualise 28

Chapter 5: Law Of Attraction 32

Chapter 6: Genuinely Elieving Or Wishful Thinking 43

Chapter 7: Understanding You 54

Chapter 8: 7 Mistakes To Avoid When Using The Powers Of Attraction To Improving Your Relationships 65

Chapter 9: How To Create Relationships, Money, Health And Careers 74

Chapter 10: Goal Setting 86

Chapter 11: Cultivating Gratitude 98

Chapter 12: Profile Of Vibration 112

Chapter 13: Love Unconditionally 125

Chapter 14: Practical Techniques In Healing The Mind 135

Chapter 15: Believing You Cannot 147

Chapter 16: Building Your Vision For Abundance 159

Chapter 17: Never Give Up 169

Conclusion 184

Chapter 1: Why It Hasn't Worked For Me Yet

The LOA seems easy enough. The LOA can be simplified to the point that you only need to concentrate on what you want. This will allow you to attract wealth, happiness, love, health and other positive outcomes. If you have ever attempted the LOA, you will see that it is not as simple as it appears. Some people do not see results even after putting in all of their effort. They might be able to make some progress, but realize they are not getting the results they desire. It does not matter if your LOA is new or familiar. Understanding the LOA will help to avoid making the same mistakes in your journey.

1) Self-destructive thoughts/beliefs

In the previous chapter we said that belief was one of the keys to activating the LOA in your life. Even though you think you want the best job, deep within you feel that your salary and job are not worthy. This happens at the subconscious level. When this happens, it causes you give off a wrong vibration. In short, your subconscious mind is blocking your efforts through unsupportive thoughts or beliefs that automatically send negative vibrations out towards the Universe.

You can think of your subconscious as your loud inner critic. You must tone down all your unsupportive and opposing thoughts. Or, "They won't ever consider me" because I'm too senior. Your subconscious mind reacts in this manner because it wants you to be safe from unknown and uncharted territories. This means that it resists change and hinders your efforts by generating self-destructive thoughts. Your subconscious mind prefers that your comfort zone is where you are most comfortable. You feel like your current job is safe, even though it's not what you want. This will cause your subconscious mind to plague you with insecurity, doubts, and fear. Simply put, this means that although your conscious has already requested the Universe for your assistance, the vibration generated by your subconscious mind due to unsupportive thought patterns is off-kilter. It is important to have a clear signal in order to achieve exactly what you desire. The vibration is what signals; being vague and unpredictable does not help vibrational alignment. The good thing is that you have complete control.

How do you stop the subconscious mind trying to undermine you? We discussed earlier that positive emotions, like love and joy, could boost our positive vibrations. You should instead of challenging negative thoughts and patterns in your subconscious mind, try harnessing positive feelings every day. Positive emotions can be a powerful tool to help you manifest your dreams. Being positive can help to squash fears, doubts, and insecurities. By replacing them, you will increase self-confidence, selfesteem and optimism. You are now ready to receive the manifestation of your desires because you no longer have contradictory thoughts. You will feel that your manifestations are on their way, and there is nothing you need to do but keep reminding God.

Suggestions:

i) Automatic Negative Thoughts

ANTs is a common term used by therapists to refer to your repeated negative thoughts. Writing down every negative thought (e.g. regrets or mistakes, fears, insecurities, etc.) on a piece is a way to counter this. Keep writing until you are done. Next, write a positive statement for every negative comment you have written. Age is just a number. This practice will help you change your perspective. Take out your negative ANTs list whenever you see yourself doing the same thing. Keep practicing until this becomes a part of your new thought process.

ii) Regular exercise

Research has shown that regular exercise can help improve mood, stress, anger, and even mild depression. Cardiovascular exercises such as swimming, running and cycling are great for improving your mood. Yoga, Tai Chi, and Qigong concentrate more on breathing.

iii. Random acts and kindness

Simple things can be done, such as holding the door for someone you don't know, holding the elevator for someone else, helping an elderly person cross the road or posting positive comments or reviews to make someone's life better. No act is too small to show kindness.

iv) Positive reinforcement

Consider bringing joy to your life with holiday souvenirs, inspirational card, potted plants, flowers, or other items that can bring you positive emotions, memories and joy.

*Note, I have more ways to feel happy every single day. Check out my book "Habits of repetitive dominant thoughts and emotions - How can you feel positive in less that 5 minutes. This will set you on the right path.

2) Law of Inspired Action

Many people mistakenly believe that the LOA involves asking the Universe for what they want and then trusting it to do the rest. You must act to reach your goals in order for the LOA system to work. This is known as Law of Inspired Action. In this divine arrangement, both you and Universe are co-creators. That means that you must take action. The Law of Inspired Action requires you to be focused on your own sphere of influence and to act from an attitude of abundance and inspiration, because you believe that it is already yours.

It is because some people become disillusioned in putting in effort to make the LOA work. They are not willing to make any effort to reach their goal so that they don't feel fulfilled. Recall the example of your dream job. If you find that you are not qualified, you make a conscious effort and enroll in part-time courses to improve your skills. You will update your resume as well as your interview skills. All of these are within your reach. The Universe however will provide opportunities for you to meet ex-colleagues who are now working at the same company and would be happy to recommend your application. You may also experience the abundance of the Universe through intuition, an inspired idea, or a lucky coincidence. Some people are content to wait and see the moment pass by without ever taking action on their ideas. Remember that the Universe is just waiting for someone to move. You have to be proactive if you want faster results.

3) Too big a jump

Many people become obsessed with the LOA when they hear it for the first time. They try to manifest millions of dollars. Their zeal quickly wore off when they realized that even though they believed it for a month, the one million dollar dream wasn't going to happen. These people did not realize that the LOA was a process for many of us. While it is possible, one million dollars can be achieved. However, most of us don't believe or have the right mindset to do so. Your subconscious mind could be reminding yourself about your almost empty bank accounts. Before the LOA can work, it is necessary to believe it. You will have to let go of any doubts, beliefs or mindsets before you can leap to the next stage. Otherwise you will become frustrated and give-up trying to force them into existence.

Tip 1: Begin small and build your confidence to be able to practice the LOA. As an example, if your income is $100,000 per year, then you can begin by trying to increase it to $20,000. Your small victories will eventually motivate and inspire you toward greater goals.

Chapter 2: Why Manifestation Didn't Work Out For You

You've followed every instruction and technique from the best mentors. Yet, you still failed. What went wrong, exactly? The answer is very simple. We have all made the exact same mistakes. Don't worry, you can change.

Let's review the below lists. You will discover one or more reasons manifesting did not work for you.

1. You are focusing on the wrong thing.

Your subconscious mind absorbs everything you see around you like it is a sponge. Although you may be focused on the thing you want, your subconscious mind will also think about things that are not in line with your wishes. The subconscious mind is much more adept at breeding negativity and positivity. LOA can channel its vibe based what your mind is focused upon - usually, the negatives.

For instance, you may want to buy a brand new BMW X7 car in 2021. Your mind is distracted by your old car. It's paint is peeling everywhere, and its engine is cracking down all the time. Your mind is focused more on your car, which can make you frustrated and angry. What about your thoughts about purchasing a new car. Your negative thoughts about your old car were more important than your positive thoughts about buying the new car. This is the reason you didn't buy your new vehicle.

2. You must decide what it is you want.

You will not get what you want, no matter how powerful or effective the LOA. The process of manifestation may slow down or stop entirely. You must be clear and vivid.

If you're short of money, for example, you might "want to have money". But you didn't specify the exact amount. The universe doesn't understand "want" money and gets confused. The universe will grant you money. It could be in the form a few dollars to a hundred bucks or even as coins. Make sure to specify how much and when you need it. It's a good idea not to spend too much at first. A few hundred or a couple thousand is an example of a small amount. Do not ask for a million bucks. If you don't get it at the exact time you asked, you will regret. Always start small. Try it out. Have fun with the universe. See what it can do. When you learn how the universe works, you can think bigger.

3. You have to believe first, and then you must receive!

If this mentality is present, you will never be able to get the results you seek. No matter how many manifestations you make, the universe will not grant you your request. Many people feel frustrated and disillusioned because they don't believe in the power of belief to manifest their desires.

The impossible is possible, so believe in it. Enjoy it and don't be stressed about it.

4. You don't have to be discouraged!

The universe will only respond to your energy vibrations. If you are desperate, your desire won't be attracted even if the universe sends vibes telling you so. Once you have a wish, you need to ask for it. After that, trust the universe. As we said in the previous section, you must believe it will come to you before it does. Indesperation can cause you to resist and not receive positive vibes. The universe will detect the resistance within you and not fulfill your request.

One good example is placing your order online via ecatalog. Let's imagine you saw a beautiful handbag. You place the order, pay and wait. You trust that the company would deliver it. As you wait for the courier to arrive, visualize the following: He knocks on your front door, hands you the parcel, and you immediately open the packaging. It made you happy to see the bag you ordered, which is gorgeous as it was presented in the ecatalog. If you are going to ask the universe any question, you need positive vibes. You can trust the universe. Believe in yourself and have faith. You can say "no" all negative thoughts and emotions. Be gentle with you.

5. You can't make excuses.

Don't excuse yourself! Stop thinking "What if", 'but I think", 'I am not certain", 'can I?

In the first paragraph, I said that if we focus on the wrong thoughts (i.e. Negative thoughts such as the ones I've just mentioned will cause negative vibes to be expressed into the universe. You will not get anything you desire. To stop thinking of negative words, you must stop. Use your word with care and make it sound positive.

6. Have fun with your thoughts and make it enjoyable!

People are too concerned about manifesting and become stressed out. Being happy can make manifesting fun. It is faster and easier to attract positive vibes.

If you already know the things you want, then trust the universe. It is easy to have fun.

7. You shouldn't be overambitious.

It is because you get too excited, and go too far. It happens to all people. If you believe in the LOA, your wish will most likely come true. Wrong! This will distract from your intentions and hinder them from manifesting.

Take the example of manifesting $10k instead than $100k.

It is possible to manifest $100k. But, some people doubt it. If you start small (say $10k), it is more feasible. When you are able to manifest your desires, your belief system, and your feelings will all be strengthened. After you have received $10k, you might be able to increase that amount.

8. You surround yourself with toxic people

Consider your surroundings, friends and family. Chances are you have at the very least one toxic family member, or even a toxic "good buddy" who loves to give negative feedback. They will not support you but instead criticize all that you do. If you want to achieve your dreams, you should stay clear of toxic people. Toxic people are always complaining, which can distract your mind, performance, or make you unhappy. This blocks the universe's ability to fulfill your desires.

9. You feel resistance

Fear from past negative experiences could make you feel resistant. Resist the negative energy, thoughts, or fear. Your life will be dominated by it. Negative vibes are more likely to attract the universe. You need to let go your fear and be grateful for what you already have.

10. You lack grateful feelings

If you're not grateful for the present, the universe wont provide what you want. The universe detects your negative vibes. Practice gratitude to transform your energy and into positive vibes. The universe will grant you all that you desire.

11. You have to believe in the universe

Put your faith in God to bring about your desired outcome. Be able to face your doubts. It can be hard for people to believe in a universe, especially when they don't know what the future holds. What can you lose by believing in the universe? There is nothing wrong with that. Do you want the universe's positive response? Have faith, trust it, be happy, enjoy life, and be thankful.

Chapter 3: Building A Strong Oneness

Oneness is something we keep hearing about, and now it's time to find out how that can happen. Any method that brings your source of power within the universe closer will create this bond. However, many people don't know where or how to begin. We will cover some of the most common methods. You are free to try as many as you like until you find your perfect match.

Clearing your mind is the most important part of creating this bond. It's difficult to find the right time in today's busy world to take your mind off of all the electronic distractions and daily life. This is how you can create a bond with the universe. It's difficult to focus for even one minute without thinking. However, with patience and practice you will discover that this peaceful place where you can connect with all things and feel one with them will transform your perspective on life. Your life will start to improve and change when you can find this oneness. The best peace and tranquility comes from being able just to exist in this moment.

Prayer is something that many people are familiar with. It doesn't matter which religion you belong to, manifesting it is not about religion. It is a spiritual awakening. This allows you to connect with a higher power, not just a brick and mortar structure. Although it is an easy way to begin praying, it does not mean that you have to stop there. While traditional prayer is about giving thanks, asking for whatever, it is usually not about reaching closer to the power of your prayers. If it were, manifesting would not be necessary as you would already be able to meet your needs. If you are new to manifesting, the concept of prayer can be used to give you an understanding of how it works. What is really different about prayer is that it is an ancient practice that teaches you that you are a weak being that does not deserve anything. You must go to a higher power and beg for all you need because you are ineligible for any good things in your life. Traditional prayer will not take you to a level of oneness and unity with your higher power.

Another technique is visualization. If the environment you live in is so chaotic that you are unable to find a quiet place to connect with God, then visualization may be able to help you locate the spot you envision as the perfect place. This can be done with practice but it is well worth it. Close your eyes. Visualize the most tranquil place you can picture. Allow yourself to relax into the peace and tranquility that surrounds you. Relax. Take a deep and slow breath. It is okay to take as long as you want to explore the world you created. But if you worry about losing yourself and you don't want to be redirected to reality, put some boundaries in place. Once you have created an environment that allows you to relax, start to reach out and ask the universe to allow you to connect with it. This should never be done while driving or performing any task that requires your attention. Otherwise, you might lose time.

The point is that time was created by man and is now controlled by him. The universe has always existed and will forever exist. It has no concept about time, unlike humans. Animals have a completely different concept of the time than humans. Animals are driven by survival instincts and not by the clock or time. This notion of time is something man created. It's something we have to live with every day. But you can end time. If you stop allowing time to be your ruler, you will enjoy your life more and have more control over your destiny. This may not be something your can do right away, or even in this month. But it can be something that you set for you and maybe something that you ask the universe. Ask any retired person about how their time perception changes when they aren't restricted by work schedules.

Meditation is a great method to clear your thoughts. Meditation can be done in many different ways. As long as you get the desired result of clearing your thoughts, all meditations are acceptable. Meditation is the art, or science, of focusing. Meditation is the art of focusing on one thing, regardless of whether it is your body or something else. It is well known that meditation can increase concentration and happiness while decreasing anxiety and stress. If meditation is something you have never done before, choosing a special time is the best way. Meditation can be done in any place you like, including sitting. Start by gently stretching your muscles. This allows your muscles to relax and helps you to focus on your own thoughts. Now, sit down or lie down and start taking slow, deep inhalations. This helps relax your muscles, slows heart rate and allows your mind focus. Keep your attention on your breathing and how you feel. If your mind drifts away from the task at issue, it is time to refocus. In the beginning, you might need to do this repeatedly until your mind becomes used to the idea. If you're still having difficulty, focus on an object (candles can have a soothing affect for most people). Meditation forces your mind to relax and requires you to pay closer attention to your body. Once you have developed a routine that allows you to relax, you are ready to be one with the universe. Time doesn't exist in this state. Relax and be with yourself. If thoughts try to interrupt your peace, you can acknowledge them and then focus on what is important, whether that's your breathing, your body, an object, or anything else.

Many people report being able to meditate when they are having trouble solving problems. Then, after a session of meditation, the answer appears to be right in front of them. Sometimes the answers we need to our problems are in us. But, our lives can make it difficult to see them. In this instance, it is also possible for the old saying to "sleep over it" to be true. The mind can be very powerful if it has the ability to slow down and take in the information as it comes. This is a separation from the conscious thinking process and the subconscious thinking process that allows the mind to find the oneness with all things. The answers that it receives are often dismissed by the mind as just coincidence. In such cases, we are unable to give credit where credit is due.

Sometimes, all we need is to slow down enough that the universe can reach out and touch our hearts. Take a few minutes to observe the wildlife outside and you will be surprised at how real-time the natural world around your. It is humans who have lost touch of the universe in our world. Because of the amazing brains we have, which process so many information, we have somehow lost touch with the source of our existence and are now miserable. It's all about us worrying about everything, from what we will eat to where we will live. Plants and animals are free from such worries. Yet, all of us were created by the powerful Creator.

Locate a place that you can interact with nature. Listen to nature's sounds as you sit down, slow and deeply. If we allow nature to touch our hearts, peace surrounds us. This peace creates a sense of oneness with the universe. It is everywhere around us all day, but it requires that we reach out to it, wish it, and feel the need to harness it for the good of all living things. It may be out there but that doesn't necessarily mean it will knock at your door asking for attention. Before anything happens, you have to put your focus on it. To do that, you must have a clear mind and not get distracted by your electronic gadgets or a to-do listing. It is hard to concentrate when everything is going on around you. The most difficult thing for many people is to do nothing for 10 minutes. During these ten-minutes, your mind will begin to think of everything you could or should be doing. This will hinder your ability build connections and connect with the Universe around you.

Give yourself permission not to worry about the day. It will all be waiting for the you, ten minutes to an hour later. If you want to create a better world, you should take the time and practice manifesting. It is important to remember that success in any area of life requires effort.

Chapter 4: How To Visualise

Visualisation is a powerful tool for manifesting your money. There are many different ways to visualize. However, the one I chose to use was the best for me. I used find law of attraction exercises in morning and evening a chore. It wasn't fun until I was actually participating in the activity. But, this visualisation technique made it so I began to look forward each day to my 'manifestation times'. I would feel like a child Christmas morning and get excited. This was exactly what I needed to experience to achieve the results I desired. I would find myself doing the same technique in down time, as if I was sitting on a train.

The Technique

It is important to imagine the experience from the first person (point-ofview) perspective. To really feel the experience, I needed my own body to see it through my own eyes. Many people visualize the experience from a third-person viewpoint, as if they were watching them on a big screen. This did not work for me. This type of visualisation was not able to give me the feeling.

However, when you have a pointofview perspective, all senses are included.

My Manifestation Dream

For me, I had an income target that I wanted to achieve. The reward for this income was that it would allow me to spend the summer in a foreign location. So every morning and evening I would begin to design my dream location'. I would imagine my apartment in this exotic spot. It was always nighttime, with a cool breeze blowing in through the large windows. I would visualize this so deeply, so indelibly, that my body and brain wouldn't even know it wasn't a real thing - YET. This would cause me to feel a cooling breeze through my body. I felt so connected to the dream that my senses could reach out and touch anything and I could feel it. I would go back to this dream scene often, and not only in the morning and afternoon. But it was the exotic location and the apartment which marked that I had reached my income goals.

With such a strong manifestation goal, there was no way it couldn't happen! I not only reached my income goals but I also blew them out of the water!!

Chapter 5: Law Of Attraction

Energy is the foundation of our world. Energy makes up our bodies, our cells, and all the atoms in the world. The strings are the basis of everything. From strings to atoms to objects, we can touch and hold physical things. Everything around and within you vibrates to certain frequencies. Even thoughts and emotions vibrate to a specific frequency. Law of Attraction speakers commonly use the expression, "To manifest your wishes, you must match yourself with the vibrational levels of the things you desire."

Manifesting your desires

There is a lot of misinformation around the Law of Attraction. So many people can say so many different things, sometimes in complete conflict with one another. I am not here trying to settle disagreements or claim who said it first. I'm here to give my opinion on this powerful and simple universal law.

To manifest your desires, your emotional vibrational frequency must match yours. You'll be able to recognize it once you align yourself properly. There will be a distinct lack in your desire for it. You'll feel deep within your soul that it's already coming to you. It's destiny. There is no way to fail. Destiny you have created.

"Never let others' fateful limitations limit your hopes and dreams. The distorted outlook of the doomspeakers and naysayers will not help you see the true path to your destiny. You should not judge others by their words. Instead, you should accept actual results as advice. Don't be surprised if there is absolutely nothing magical or miraculous about the reality that you witness from those who are eagerly to assist you. Friends and relatives who feel the absence of joy, love or prosperity in their own lives are not allowed to place their limitations on your reality.

-- Anthon St. Maarten

You are not what you want

You're not in alignment when you sit and think about what you want. Your desire for it, whatever it may be, will keep it away from you. When you lose the feeling that you desire something, manifestation can happen quickly and powerfully.

If you feel excited, it is an indication that you are in alignment to your desires. It is that feeling when you place your order at your favorite eatery and the server brings it to you. There was no need to worry about if you did it right, or if it would be delivered. It was easy to ask, and within minutes you would receive the answer. The Law of Attraction works similarly. You streamline the process by focusing on what you want and not on how it will happen. (God. The Universe. Your Higher Self. Whatever you would like to credit for helping in your manifestations.

Reality is made from consciousness

In quantum physics, it's a well-known notion that our thoughts influence the world around. Each person's perception of reality is different, and this is no accident. Each person has a different perception of reality and therefore no two realities will be alike.

It is a common belief that consciousness creates reality. This leads to many questions. Does this mean we, both individually and collectively, can create and modify reality as we wish? Could we possibly create certain lifestyles? How long does it take to manifest? It is difficult to know how long it will take.

Everything we see, all of our thoughts and reality are vibrating on a vibrational basis. Also, our thoughts have their vibrational frequency. Aligning our thoughts with our wishes will help us see the desired result in our lives. Mastering mindfulness through meditation is the first step toward seeing your desires flourish before you.

Quantum Double Split Experiment

This is a popular experiment that proves there is a connection between consciousness and the real world. The study concluded that consciousness-related factors are strongly linked to the double slit interference. Parapsychology studies and experiments have also confirmed this phenomenon.

Our minds create the world around ourselves, either by simply observing it from a different perspective or manipulating it through manifestations and attraction. Similar experiments include the global conscious theory, which claims that we are all one consciousness. One mind can experience different realities at different times. Also, thoughts and feelings can alter the structure water. These topics are beyond my scope, but I won't dwell on them here.

Action

I have provided many suggestions throughout this book to help you take the first steps towards achieving your dreams. Meditation allows you to change the way that you think and how you communicate with yourself. All those chapters, all that knowledge is the prequel. This is where all of that comes together. This is where it all comes together.

In this final section I'll demonstrate how to use all of the information in this book to improve your life. Your thoughts are what will make your life better. Keep your focus on the positive and the good, and be grateful for all that is possible. You can be supportive of your positive thoughts by gently letting go of the negative ones after careful analysis. The second important thing is what you do to get your desired results.

Law of Attraction speakers can tell you that you don't need to think negatively, have positive feelings and focus your attention on your desires. Your desire will soon come. While those are good mindsets, they fail to mention the crucial aspect. You must take action to achieve your goal. It is not possible to change your current situation by staying put.

Are you able to see Attraction in all its forms? ACTION. Without action, it's just wishful-thinking. It's like a child who wishes on a shootingstar. That's all it does, is to plant the seed and tell the universe what you want. It is a major slap in their faces. You cannot expect to be successful, make your money and achieve your desires if nothing is done. Thinking positively and visualizing are important, but not enough.

After you've completed your steps, get in the zone of manifesting your goals. This sets the stage for you to take inspired action. What is inspiration action? They could be called hunches. They will appear suddenly and you'll notice them. Sometimes you'll be able to notice them and let them go, but it won't do any good. It's better to take action than dream, if you don't want to stop wishing.

For instance, if you have a desire to own a car then go to a dealership. Would you like to be a well-known writer? Take note of the ideas that you get, regardless of how brief. It's the same as trying to win in the lottery. You will never win if the urge to buy a lottery ticket is ignored.

Now that we've covered the idea of inspiration leading to action, what does it mean for someone to know whether their thought or idea has been "inspired"? There are many ways you can tell, especially when you're truly in touch with your emotions and thoughts by practicing mindfulness and meditation.

1. Inspired action makes you feel good. It will make you feel passionate, happy, and excited. It's possible to think or act from a place of inspiration, love and joy. Fear, jealousy, insecurity, or fear are the reasons behind an "ego"-based action. To avoid something you don't enjoy, you might do something.

2. It's comfortable. You feel at home in this behavior. There is no other place in the world that can make you feel so at-home. If you are impatient or jealous, it is counterintuitive to achieving your goals.

3. It's fun! It's fun! Everything will make complete sense.

4. It's unexpected. The random thought you have in the shower or on your way to work. A "ego"-based action is motivated by the desire to plan, find the details, and try to predict every outcome. When you just let it go, manifestation begins.

5. It comes from the space of allowing. You allow your desires to come into your life. A "ego-based action" is one that is attached to the result. The moment you release your attachment to the outcome and let go, everything will fall into your hands and you will see your life change.

By putting your intentions into action, you show the universe that you really want it. If they don't see immediate results, self-deprecating thoughts of failing slip into the minds of many. This is why meditation is so crucial to your success and being a successful manifestor. Action is simply another manifestation, the manifestation or the energy that you want.

We too often see our opportunity as a carrot tied to a string. But we don't always take it. Fear of failure or rejection, being too stuck in our daily lives or being too complacent, makes it difficult to pursue our passions. Instead of following our path, we keep walking. Too often, our fears or insecurity prevent us form chasing these dreams and from making progress towards them.

It's important for us to remember that whatever we put our mind to, anything is possible. Keep your thoughts positive. You can use meditation to calm your mind, as well as your emotions. Don't miss out on any opportunities that may come your way. All of these will help you live happier and more fulfilling lives, even if the manifestations aren't immediate.

Chapter 6: Genuinely Elieving Or Wishful Thinking

The LOA has been a huge success. It is shocking to me that so many people still believe it. However, I was able to learn from people why this is. These three elements are the root cause of The Law of Attraction not being effective for individuals.

1) Most people won't accept everything about themselves, which is why the Law of Attraction is so valid. It is crucial to trust in it fully for it not to fail.

2) People who trust it are not fully aware of its functions. There are some things that perform a huge job because of how it works. Additionally, although people may be aware of what these things are, they do not know how to use them.

3) The LOA stockholders don't really know how to recognize or perceive the answers they receive to their inquiries or

solicitations. We must not fail to grasp the necessary responses that The Universe offers.

Now, I will be making a valiant attempt to tell you how to know when God/The Universe is talking to you and how you can understand what He's trying to share with you. The Law of Attraction works best when you focus on the core principles (thinking, feeling, envisioning and accepting). These simple steps don't work when people try them. People typically only notice a few small results by following this method. You may find that they see more unexpected events or are closer to your goals. These people never achieved what they needed because they didn't follow all of their explicit directions. Although they claim they have faith, the truth is that they don't. They might need to believe in The Law of Attraction since they have seen it work for others. It is possible that some of these individuals have actually seen the Law of

Attraction work for them. If not, they simply chalked it all up to fate. Be that though, intuition tells them they still have questions. It doesn't really matter how many times those questions remain. They won't be able use the Law of Attraction in these circumstances. There are also those, like my better halves, who believe that trusting and wishing is equivalent to acceptance. My better halves consistently affirms that the LOA works. Unfortunately, the announcement has a consistent problem.

For example my better half complains a lot that he doesn't have the option of saving money or about his long commute. I remind him of Law of Attraction, and help him remember that his whining about money is only creating more cash saving problems for himself. My significant other, regardless his drive or money issues, is a cheerful person. He is a joy and makes people laugh. He loves his children to death and gives them all the love they deserve when he goes home.

Although he only has a few issues, he can't help but to harp about them.

Harping about an issue is the worst thing you could do. My better half will cover the tabs until my stomach is full. He tells me that it is true. There is no reason anyone shouldn't feel this way about anything. It is a fact that the more you feel into an idea the better it turns out. This includes everything you are concerned or worried about. The situation will only worsen if it is already obvious.

It's terrible to take care tabs. It is important to make an effort to not let it get in the way of your daily life. You must take care of it so there's no reason to get upset. It won't change your current situation. It won't change your circumstances. If you get frustrated, try to be grateful for the administration you have paid for. If you feel angry about the amount of power bills you are currently paying and you begin to realize how many people must accept this law and some truly believe it is too high, then try to think internally "Well, at all rates, we have strength." I'm grateful we have that power. Consider that you may have the funds to cover the cost of that tab.

I know of other people who have written the words, "Thank You for administrations rendered" or (whatever the administration was). They simply write it on the bill and put it in the mail with the check. Brain science has a lot to do with this. This will be a great pace for later appreciation classes. My partner lives a difficult existence. He will need to drive between 2 and 4 hours each day. He will then need to work between 8-10 hour days of hard physical labor. He walks into the home of three children when he comes back from another long drive. The only thing the poor person has to do is relax on the loveseat. Indeed, his situation is extremely troubling. But, it doesn't have to be that way. I try to explain to him that we could draw closer to his works. It is possible.

I know he has great credit, and we own our house. It is possible to do it. Be that it may, he continued to state, "We just can't get closer." It's inconceivable. I would prefer not having a larger mortgage on my house. I don't own this; I don't possess that, Blah. I have several ideas for how we might get closer. Regardless of this, my better halves will never doubt that there is some problem with the arrangement.

Instead of saying, "I don't' have the cash", he should be saying, "WHEN you have the capital, we'll move, and it'll be amazing!" My significant other is the best man I know. He is my best friend. He has a rare activity, he is extremely wealthy, and he works tirelessly. In any event, he must be honest about his goals and stop telling himself that he doesn't have the time. He should be more close to work and start to believe that it will happen. Only when he is able to see the positive outcomes, things will change in his favor. I often hear my significant other say, "Kid you sure have an incredible life, don't ya?" in a humorous tone. I simply put my feet on the ground, smile and say to him, "Why yes, I do."

The Law of Attraction allows you to find the wonderful side of any given circumstance. In fact, every given moment has a bright side. My better half hates driving, which I have already stated. I suggest to him that he listen to audiobooks or the radio. Are you aware of what he tunes out to while driving home from work? He tunes into TV programs about money, the economy. It's not surprising that he is so critical of his drive. I instruct him to be mindful of the fact that he has some private time before he returns to us. It should be his break before he comes back to work. It is possible to see the bright side. It takes practice, preparation, repetition, but it is possible.

Many people are highly motivated employees with high standards. A few people have big dreams and expectations.

They are also impractical learners. These are remarkable characteristics. But, this is not how genuine acceptance works. The Law of Attraction doesn't mean trusting and hoping. It's an astonishing inverse. You don't need to ask for it to happen. It is essential to know that it will happen. To be able to live your dreams is a right. However, not all people who clutch dreams have the same thing. They also hold onto all the reasons their fantasies won't happen. What I mean is the dream. They keep reminding themselves that it hasn't been realized at this point, and all the reasons why.

These individuals are likely to believe that only having high expectations is enough to attract The Law of Attraction. They are losing their overall purpose. It is okay to be a skeptic, but it will not get you closer towards your goals. Wishing and knowing can be two different things. Cynicism is another thing that will keep you from achieving the goals you set. Cynicism is a way to keep your life from falling apart. As a matter fact, this is what will happen to you. The LOA and Negativity lie at the edges of the field. Remove all cynicism. You'll be amazed at how many positive outcomes you can achieve just by making one small move. It is not easy to be positive while still trusting in The Law of Attraction.

Acceptance is the way to every part of daily life. You must take every step necessary to be a success in any endeavor. You will see that all we think will happen will become reality. You might have the faith to believe in The Law of Attraction and still be able to ask questions. You may discover that there are times when you truly have faith in it and then there are other times when you don't. If you absolutely need to believe that the LOA is true, you should use the LOA for support and guidance. Let those moments that you do accept go and let them run. When you have faith in it, you can get excited about the idea and express gratitude towards The Universe for helping to bring forth The Law of Attraction. Everyone asks questions occasionally. The question isn't about whether The Law of Attraction works. But, every now and again, when we realize that it does, we are able to ask ourselves whether we can make the dreams come true. This is normal, especially if this is your first time using The Law of Attraction.

The Law of Attraction is a tool that will assist you in believing in it, your fantasies, and more. Be grateful for the moment when you reach full confidence and then ask The Universe to give you more faith. Gradually you will begin to gain more confidence over time. Your fantasies will come true if there is more confidence. You don't have to do this every minute you spend putting money into it. Don't do this while you feel like it. You can't fool The Universe. The Universe cannot be deceived. This will cause you to feel more uncertainty.

Chapter 7: Understanding You

How well do your skills and knowledge of yourself compare to others?

Ask most teenagers this question and you will get a blank look. Ask a twentysomething for the same answer and you will get an almost arrogant, confident response. Ask a twenty-something and they'll give you a variety of answers.

Ask someone in their sixties to seventies and you'll find confidence. You will become more wise as you age. The more you grow in wisdom, the more you discover what you don't know. In other terms, when you are young, you assume you have all the answers. As you grow older, you realize just how wrong you were. You will experience a period of transition where you will discover your innermost desires and nature.

It's about getting to know yourself. You might be young now, or you may be in your

40s/50s/50s or even older. It's never too late or too soon to find out who and how you are.

The first step towards changing the energy surrounding you is to understand yourself. Negative energy will surround you if you are arrogant. Arrogance means being cocky and confident without having any substance. Arrogance does not make you a good artist.

Lebron James is a prime example. Many would claim that he was arrogant. While still playing high school football, he was highly considered for the NBA. He was instantly drafted to the pros after high school.

His arrogance prompted 'The Decision to Leave' his Cleveland Cavaliers home team. This led to him being ridiculed by many. It wasn't because of him leaving, but rather how he had left. His arrogance cost many fans and would-be supporters. He found so many people disliking him and rooting for him that it was clear it was bothering Him during his first season in the Miami Heat.

He went on to win 2 championships and reach the finals in all four seasons with the Miami Heat. However he did change after the first season. He became a stronger leader for the team, and his arrogance turned into confidence. Positive things started to happen when he did that.

Let's learn more about you.

What you need.

This topic was discussed in the final chapter. But what should you do?

Are you unsure if you can attract anything?

"Well I do want to have a good family and a nice house, but where is that?"

If you cannot be clear about your goals, or if you lack the confidence to make them a reality, then you are presenting a blurred idea to the universe.

What if you told yourself that you would love to someday own a house? Something decent. And then, thirty years later, managed to buy a home near your job in a terrible part of town. Is that what you really wanted?

Or was it? Let's have a closer look.

You will one day own a home. The day you want to own your home is not far off. So is 40, 50 and 60. Maybe you'd be annoyed if it took so long for you to buy something. You're not being specific.

Next, what you wanted was 'decent. The universe isn't able to tell the difference. If you don't specify, you're leaving it open to interpretation.

The expression "Not too close" is also open to interpretation. Not too far from where you work? You don't have to go far. 10 miles? 30? 100? Not far from the ocean? Family? Your hometown

Being indecisive, tentative, or unsure is not going provide you with much positive energy. It's almost like you don't think you can achieve what you really want. Or that you don't deserve it.

You will think negatively if you think like that.

Stop it. It must stop immediately.

Be confident. Get clear on what you want.

If that seems too difficult because you aren't happy with so many things, you can always start with the ones you don't want.

Don't get what you don't want.

There are always many things you don't desire. Debt. A bad relationship. Negative people. Jealous people. So on.

Take a look at all the things you don't need. It could be a high-ranking position in a company. Or, it could mean working at the local diner.

Whatever it is, make a note of it. This will show you a pattern and help you avoid getting what is not really yours.

You might begin to see some of the things you are seeing around you. It may be time to get rid of people who make you unhappy, cause you distress, or are just too dependent. This could include friends you have known for many years, family members, and even your partner.

You don't need to be close to them right now. But you must identify the things you don't wish in your life.

How to discover your true inner desires.

With all of the possibilities and ideas that life offers, it can feel overwhelming to decide what your true desires are.

You probably knew your goals at one point in time. Then your life got chaotic. Then, you found yourself with new responsibilities.

All this external noise blocks your true desires.

It is important to go to a quiet area to help you get rid of the noise. If you live alone, you can use your own home as a quiet place or choose a room within it. Turn off all distractions. Make sure that everyone knows that you will need to be quiet for a while.

You can begin to look back at your life from your teenage years through today once you're in that peaceful place. Consider all of the possible careers or professions you could imagine.

Note them.

Next, think back to the ideal relationship you saw when you were younger. Talking to someone with the opposite sexual orientation was nerve-racking for you. Was it the most important thing in your life?

Were their looks the reason? Did it have to do with their smile? Was it their smile or the kindness they showed to people, especially those who were being picked on? Is it because they were responsible

What are your priorities right now? Are you after the 'hot looking' girl or boy? Are you looking for someone who's 'dangerous,' or a 'bad' person?

Why would you do such a thing? Do you seek adventure? You are looking for someone to be better. Many people believe that they can fix the other person. They're not the ones to change. Instead, they chase people who they believe are 'broken'. When it becomes obvious that they can no longer change the other person's mind, the relationship is ruined.

Write down what is important to you about a relationship.

Then you can begin to look at your living situation. What kind of home would be the most comfortable? Do you think it would be a house in a rural environment? Are you near water, like the ocean, river, or lake? Do you ever wish to live in another country? Why?

What number of bedrooms would you require? What kind or number of neighbors would suit you?

The more details you can remember now, you'll be more precise. Your positivity will increase if your details are precise.

It's important to learn all about it.

Clear vision is key to attracting the things you desire. If you aren't clear on things, your energy will be negative.

Also, don't be unclear about your desires. If you don't get what you want you might not be content with them for a while.

The clutter in your life, whether it's in the form or confusion, must be cleared away. Clearer you can attract more prosperity into your life.

Then, you'll start to notice all the other wonderful things going on around you.

You'll be amazed how you managed to survive.

You know what that is, my friends? A wonderful feeling. You can bet that I can!

Chapter 8: 7 Mistakes To Avoid When Using The Powers Of Attraction To Improving Your Relationships

You are trying to improve your relationship with the power of attraction. It could be that you are looking to attract a friend or ex-partner, or to bring joy back into your current relationship. You don't want to make the same mistakes as others when using attraction for better romance.

The power of manifestation won't work for you if your actions and thoughts are detrimental to its effectiveness. This list of mistakes can hinder your ability to attract the kind of romantic partner you want.

1. Not being thankful enough is a common mistake in practicing the law o attraction to attract love. This power all boils down to gratitude. If you don't feel grateful for what is available, then you may attract unwelcome or negative energy. When you start to practice gratitude, you may need to have a new attitude.

Be sure to truly express gratitude to the universe. If you do that, you will see the universe as generous enough to give you whatever you ask for. Positive thinking is a good thing for both you and the universe. When you wake up each morning, give thanks to the universe for giving you the gift that is life.

If you're blessed with the opportunity to view or hear something wonderful, please make it a point that you thank the universe. Do this daily and you'll see that the universe is slowly granting your request to attract your love.

2. Poor patience - If your impatience makes it difficult to attract love and romance, you'll be most likely to fail. Do not believe that attraction is a magic bullet. Keep in mind that the universe cannot give you your ideal man/woman within a few seconds.

Although the law emphasizes attracting what your heart desires, there is no precise timeframe for reaching your goals. Don't rush to attract what you want. Be patient. This virtue can help you achieve the best results.

Be patient with the universe. Otherwise, it will only send you negative vibes. If this happens, the universe might immediately suspend your request. That is something you do not want.

3. Not being specific enough. If you don't specify your desires, it could cause you to have to change your mind too often. This is bad for romance and true love. It can confuse the universe if your mind changes frequently. It can also make it harder to fulfill your dreams.

Before you create anything, be sure to fully understand what you desire. List all that you want in your partner or lover. Once you have compiled the list, go through it once more and pick only the things that appeal to your heart.

So that you can truly manifest the inner you, go deep down. If it is necessary to alter what you have already achieved, avoid doing so.

4. It is easy to have little faith and expect the power of attraction not to work. You need to believe in the outcome of what you create so that it happens. So that your dream romance is possible, you should have no doubts.

You don't need to get discouraged if it fails your first time. Continue to manifest until your desire for love is fulfilled. Be aware that the power and attraction of love does not always work the first attempt. This is especially true for those who make frequent mistakes.

The first thing you can do to increase your chances of success with the power of attraction is to build your faith. Believe it.

Your faith must be so solid that you can never doubt your convictions.

5. Your beliefs conflict with your desires. You can have your manifestations drastically affected if your beliefs and desires conflict. Be sure to align your desire with your belief if you are going to get something. You can create a limiting beliefs that act as mental blocks in your subconscious mind if there is a conflict. This limiting belief may limit or prevent you from realizing your dreams and desires.

If you try to attract the woman of your dreams but are always afraid and unattractive, you have already created a problem. Because of this belief, you are unable to attract all that you want, regardless how many times you meditate, use affirmations, and visualize.

This means there is a higher likelihood that the universe will give what you believe rather than what is in your heart. Before you start manifesting, it is important that you examine all of your beliefs. These beliefs must be discarded if they hinder your ability or desire to attract the life you want. Be sure to not mix your wants and beliefs.

6. Passion and passion are two things that can hinder your ability to attract the right partner. Although the process is not complicated, it takes effort. You will make mistakes, but it shouldn't stop you from trying again.

It is important to assess how much effort and time you are currently investing in your goal of finding the perfect partner before you make any decisions. Are you spending money and time trying to imitate those who achieved success in this area of life? Consider your normal thoughts. Is it your job, your loneliness or the bills?

If you feel that there are too many negative things in your life, it is time to remove them. To make the universe match your efforts, you must put in effort to manifest your dream partner. It is important to remember that while it takes effort to build a relationship, there are many benefits.

To attract your dream partner, your passion must be strong. The universe is always willing to give you the same amount of energy as you are.

7. Do not put off taking action. You can't just wish and hope. It is also about taking the steps that will help you reach your goals. Instead of wishing and hoping, you have to be the part.

To attract a partner, improve yourself in every aspect of your life. Get fitter and more active outdoors.

Do not neglect to make improvements in your life. You won't attract anything you don't want. People don't want to be attracted to someone with negative traits. It is important to work on your personality as well so that the universe can give you what you want.

Inspiring action is essential. This requires that you listen to your inner voice in order to start attracting the positive events and synchronicities into your life. You should also make an effort to go out sometimes, especially if you live in a location where your ideal companion is. By doing so, you can show the world that you are working hard to realize your dreams.

The power of attraction is truly one of the most powerful laws that has ever been introduced to mankind. It is able to attract any kind of person or thing you desire. This will make your dreams come true, particularly in your love life. Unfortunately, this is one of the areas that people make most mistakes in. Most common mistakes include negativity.

It is possible to deal with them if one focuses on being aware and fully aware about their own thoughts, actions, and emotions. You must also be open to change and improvement. If you do this, you can maximize and harness all the power of God when it comes time to creating your ideal romance.

Chapter 9: How To Create Relationships, Money, Health And Careers

You can make any wish come true. If you believe in yourself, you will attract it. Focusing on the positives and only focusing on them will help you get rid of negative vibes about your finances, career, and relationships.

The Law of Attraction is a powerful tool to manifest abundance in your life. Gratitude journals, positive affirmations and the Law of Attraction are all powerful tools.

1. Healthy Loving Relationships

It is important to change your mindset to attract love. Positive thinking will help you create a happy, successful relationship.

It doesn't matter how bad your relationship with your partner was! Consider it a learning experience. Learn from it and strive to become a better person. Realize that being positive is difficult because you're probably hurting deeply and your life seems to have crashed. I advise you to get out all your emotions and let them out. Next, get up and take a warm bath. Now, you can start thinking about your future. It is important to remember not to be focused on the negative thoughts. The sadness, frustration, anger and hatred you feel inside will not attract good vibes into your daily life. Your wishes will not come true. While I know it's difficult, it takes a strong desire to change your mindset. It took me months and many trials to finally change my mind. I was struggling, feeling depressed and frustrated every day. But, I kept telling myself that I was the only one who was suffering from this.

Finally, my decision was to make me strong. I continued fighting the negative parts of myself and kept sending positive vibes. This process went on until I realized my newfound strength and was more open-minded, braver and bolder than I thought. I will keep all negative thoughts out of my life. If I have to deal with problems, I will treat them as a challenge.

What are the characteristics you seek in your dream partner? Someone who is loving, caring. Only focus on the positive characteristics listed above to help you realize your dreams. You must believe in the universe and have patience to find the right partner for you.

How to manifest, so the Universe understands your needs

* Visualize your partner and you having happy times together.

* Practice affirmations daily. To manifest positive vibes, and a healthy marriage, you must always think positively.

* Be precise and crystal clear about what you are looking for. Note down the traits

that you look for in a partner. Looking good, attractive, wealthy, kind? Also indicate how you want your partner to treat you. Passionate, compassionate, loved?

* Make sure what you believe is consistent with your goals.

* Be open-minded to love, accept, and enjoy your new partner. Never let self-doubt defeat you. Daily affirmations are the best way to increase your vibes, align it with your request, and to make yourself feel better.

* Trust in the universe

Trust in the universe and it will bring it to you at the right time. Don't obsess over it. Instead, you should practice gratitude and affirmation. The Chapter 4 list contains suggestions on how to manifest your desires. Keep in mind the details. Understand that the universe works in your favor to speed up the process. You continue living your happy life while waiting for your ideal partner. You might be tempted to envy or feel sad when you look at a happy couple. To avoid these feelings, be positive and happy for them. If you start to think negatively, your universe will detect it and not help. You might attract the wrong person into you life. Remember that you can attract the love and partner of your choice!

* Do something about it

Do you seek a relationship that is fun, loving and supportive? This is what you have to do. Make your thoughts a reality by being kind, loving and caring to others. This helps you communicate your expectations.

* Know that you will feel more disappointed if your expectations don't materialize. You want to control how things turn out when you have an expectation. However, the universe will decide. We do not know the answers to your questions. I cannot emphasize enough the importance of manifesting and following all steps correctly

so that the universe understands you and offers you exactly what it needs (or perhaps something better). The bottom line is to trust the universe.

2. Manifest money

It is possible to have a negative view of money. You can change that perception by seeing it as something positive. You must create a positive connection between your thoughts and money. The universe will eventually provide the money for you miraculously if you feel you already have it.

Follow these steps to succeed. Ask the Universe for more money. Have a positive outlook and believe in the universe.

* Change your negative perception of money to something better Your money is a blessing. It can bring joy, give you a better life, and even help people in dire need. You can then apply the steps of manifestation to improve your money mindset and generate extra money using LOA.

* To be able to have abundance, you must visualise your money. Imagine your life after you have achieved your financial goals. Keep picturing and visualizing.

* Don't forget to trust the universe for what you need before you get it. It is essential to show gratitude in order for the universe to expedite the process. Be grateful to your health, the people in your life who love and support you, the money available for you and your family.

* Start by achieving a modest amount of money, such as $5K or $10K. This is not to be confused with $100K. This is to not set high expectations and be disappointed when you do not achieve that amount. While it is possible for $100K to be manifested, some people can even make $1,000,000.00. A beginner is more likely to be impatient and anxious than they should be, so they get frustrated when they don't get the results they desire. Then they lose heart and believe manifesting and LOA are

scams. Now you can see why it is best for you to take baby step. Once you have received a small amount of money you can increase it as much you like.

3. Manifest Health

For health manifestation, you'll use the same methods as how you manifest money or relationship. Yes, you can achieve vibrant health with the LOA.

Your subconscious mind needs to be trained to believe that you are in the best of health. It will take effort and perseverance to reprogram your subconscious mind in order to create positive energy. You will have the best health if your body is positive about your emotions. When you think in love, hope, or gratitude, your body will naturally feel positive and energetic vibes that will promote good health.

There are many methods that can help you achieve good health.

* Make positive affirmations about your health before you go to bed. Your subconscious mind can take in any thought you make. This "tricks your subconscious mind" to think positively. Practice affirmation before going to sleep is the best time.

* Don't go back to bed if you are feeling depressed, sad, angry, or depressed. Get to bed happy, peaceful, and content. Before you go to bed, practice gratitude. It helps to create stability in your body so you can feel relaxed, calm, and positive. It can even lower your blood pressure. This positive feeling will boost your energy levels the next morning.

4. Manifest Career

Are you frustrated that no offers come in for the dream job you want? There is always rejection after rejection. It makes you sad, angry, jealous, and frustrated to see your colleagues and friends celebrating the acceptance or promotion in the company they applied for.

This is the ideal time to begin a new career.

* Be vivid about the things you want

* Only focus on one job that you are interested in achieving. If you are considering a promotion to a managerial position to increase your salary, it is best to concentrate on creating the new role, not the promotion.

To make sure you have the right career path, you need to do your research. It is possible to contact an employee of the company, or search it online.

Before you start manifesting, ask these questions:

- What is your dream job position?

Is it going to make my life happy and fulfilled?

Do you think I will be excited to go to work and to see my colleagues if I get the job?

- Are your thoughts holding back you?

What steps should you take to achieve your goal?

- What skills should be acquired to improve my own abilities?

Whom should I seek advice regarding my job?

-Will I be surrounded by negative people? If so, how do I deal? If I am offered a job, will I be willing or able to get rid of these harmful people in my life?

We are all humans. The majority of us were brought up in a negative world, which caused us to focus on the negative instead of seeing the positive side and finding solutions. It is essential to focus our attention on the bright side and avoid negative influences so our brains don't become distracted.

Keep positive, be positive, and keep your focus on the job that you are interested in. Positive emotions and energy can be amplified when you feel positive about it. You can do positive visualization and affirmations every day or create a visionboard. These exercises can help reduce negative thoughts and disorientation. Final, take action. If you keep your mind open, chances are that the right opportunities will suddenly come along.

Chapter 10: Goal Setting

A goal can be defined as a desired outcome or vision that a person or organization plans to achieve. Many people's only goals are New Year's resolutions that are quickly forgotten by January 15. However, when you examine the most successful people you will see that they had goals that they worked towards. A goal is an external representation that a person has of their desires. It's not difficult to set goals but the success of executing them is incredible. Sometimes, goals are expressed in terms of the end result that one wants. This could be to lose weight or travel, or even purchase an object such as a laptop.

There are two types, performance-based goals or task-based, of goals. A task-based or performance-based goal will focus on the activities that the individual is interested in performing. Performance-based goal, on the other side, focuses on the goals that the individual is trying to achieve.

It is often more effective to set task-based than performance-based targets. This is because you are in control of your actions, but you don't have control over your performance. This is often the main reason so many New Year Resolutions fail. Many people who set New Year's resolutions to lose weight discover that they don't have any control over how fast they can accomplish this. People who have set goals to exercise more often per week than others can gauge their success or failure and are therefore better equipped to keep to their goals.

Why goals are important

You can't reach any destination if your location isn't known. Let's imagine that you would like to visit a National Park a few hours away. This is your goal. Now that you know where you want, you can buy the right map, pack the items you need, put aside the money you believe will be necessary to make the trip, as well as organize how to get there. Knowing where you want to go will lead to all of these things. It is important to have a goal. This will clarify your future goals.

There are many resources you can find that will provide the information you require to reach your goals. Here are some key points to keep in mind when setting your goals.

Your goals must be balanced. You should set goals that allow you to grow and change your entire life. Not just your career or personal health goals. If they focus solely on their own lives, they may not be as happy with their achievements. Imagine a rich lawyer or CEO who pursued his career goals at great cost to his relationships and wealth.

While he may attain the career success and wealth he craves, he may not have close friends or family to celebrate his achievements with or spend his wealth on. He may also need to channel some of his wealth toward medical bills. It is possible to have more fun by setting goals in the areas that are most important to you. One of the greatest regrets of those who have died is the fact that they worked too hard, often at the expense their health or their relationships. Here are some categories to think about when setting your goals.

* Health, well-being

* Family and Relationships

* Careers and work

* Money and property

* Creativity through experiences

It is essential to clarify your goals, and why you want them. It's helpful to clearly define what your goals are. It is easier to discern between worthwhile goals and unworthy goals if you include the reason for your goal. Writing down your goals will be the best way for you to define them. It is easier to analyze your goals if they are written down.

It's important to reflect upon your goals and be introspective. Sometimes people write down their goals only to discover that they are unrealistic. Or that they are not going to lead to the success and wealth desired. Your life purpose, your vision, or your mission must always guide your goals.

You can break down your goals and create actionable plans. Once you have your goals written down you will be able to break them up into steps that are easy for you to follow. How do we eat an elephant. One bite at each. It doesn't make a difference how ambitious your goals are. They should be both measurable, and achievable. Before you can create an actionable strategy, think about how you will measure success. You will then need to determine how you will get there. Once you know your weekly goals, you will be able to establish daily routines and habits to support you in reaching them. Setting daily routines allows you to make progress each day towards your goal. They also give you something to stick to.

You can set deadlines, track your progress, or schedule your time. If you have an end in mind, you need to decide on a reasonable date. This will help to identify and define your weekly/monthly and yearly milestones. It is also possible to split your goals into short and long term goals by setting deadlines. These are the key to scheduling your time.

Some people decide to determine a minimum amount of hours they want to spend working on their goals each week. Others set daily time blocks to achieve their goals. This will help you develop routines that you can follow each day and every week to help you meet your milestones. Tracking your progress is only possible if you have the ability to measure it. These time blocks are a great tool for tracking your progress. You can track your progress and be motivated to maintain the momentum.

It is sometimes necessary to create a working environment that supports your goals. For example, if your goal is to work on one project every day at a specific hour, you can find a private place and get rid of any distractions to ensure you are productive. So that you are always ready to go, you can also anticipate your daily needs. It could be after lunch. In this case, you can plan ahead and ensure that you eat. If you have to, you can ask to turn off your phone so you don't get distracted. Your environment can support you in reaching your dreams or cause unnecessary distractions which can then lead to missing milestones.

Importance of Goals

As I mentioned earlier, setting a goal feels like having a plan. Goals provide direction and guidance. They give you a sense of direction and help you know what you have to do in order to realize your dreams. Other than this, having goals has many other benefits.

Goals direct your focus. Many people wander aimlessly through their lives, reacting to circumstances and never seeing the potential they have. When you set a goal, it allows you to prioritize what is important and what doesn't. This helps you stay focused. If, for example, your goal is not to spend a lot of time on television, but creating a business with friends, your time will be better spent reading and researching about how to make the business successful. You will put your efforts into activities that are going to help you achieve your goals.

Goals help in decision making. When you set a goal, you can make clear decisions about the direction you want your life to go. Healthy people will be more able to refuse friends' invitations to eat out or to exercise. When you make a commitment to taking steps towards your goal it removes a lot of the struggle and willpower involved in decision-making. The day is full of decisions. But if you have clear goals and a goal to reach, then some decisions will be easier.

Goals can substitute for motivation. Sometimes, we do not feel like doing the things that we know are necessary. Many times, we don't feel like making the right decisions or following the right habits to achieve our goals. There is no way to feel motivated to exercise every day. And there are few people who would rather read a business management manual than a new novel. If you set a goal of being healthy, you will remember that you chose the vegetables and that you are reading that book because you want to achieve that goal. Reviewing your milestones each day will help you make better decisions.

You can prioritize your life by setting goals. When you have clear goals to work towards, you will be better equipped to prioritize your actions for maximum productivity.

Although the tasks involved in achieving your goals can be difficult, they are often rewarding. You can make better decisions if you know why your doing the tasks. You can prioritize the tasks that are most important to you in order to achieve your goals. While this doesn't mean that you shouldn't enjoy the things that make you happy, it means that you can begin your day with tasks that are essential to your goals and take less responsibility when you have some time to unwind and enjoy your day.

You can use goals to create momentum. Newton's law says that an object remains stationary unless it encounters an unbalanced forces. This law can be applied in life as well as to the pursuit for success. If you don't set goals, it is possible to be considered as an object at ease. Setting goals is the only way to make progress on any of your dreams. Your goals are the unbalanced force driving you to make progress. If you focus on your goals, you can begin to make progress towards them. Once you see progress you will not want stop because you want to see more.

There are other benefits to goals, too:

* Goals give hope and confidence that your goal can be achieved

* Goals assist in defeating procrastination

* Goals can help you achieve self-mastery as well as the fulfillment of all your potential

* Goals help you to define the life you truly want.

* Goals are a way to learn how you can discipline yourself and manage your emotions

* Goals encourage positive habits

* Goals are a way to improve your quality of life. Progress in one area can encourage progress elsewhere.

If you want to make positive changes in your life, then it is crucial that you clearly define your goals and create actionable steps. Success does not happen by chance. It takes effort to make your life successful. Set your goals as the first step. These goals will help you stay focused and give you direction. This will increase your chances for success. Make a conscious effort to reach your goal.

What do your goals for your life? Write it down in a task-oriented fashion and then break it apart so that you can see how you can achieve it.

Chapter 11: Cultivating Gratitude

It's possible that you will feel discouraged at times. If that happens, you may not be using the magical combination between gratitude and the law or attraction.

This is a critical step in your efforts to use the law and attract good things. Because it's so simple, most people forget about this. They get so wrapped up in the visualization and creating lists that they forget to remember that this is as important as the rest. Even if gratitude is something they keep in mind, it can lead to them doing things wrong.

Remember that manifestation relies on vibrations. You attract what you vibrate at. It means that you attract people who are down, sad or depressed. That is why gratitude can become a powerful tool. It can increase your vibrations even if you are going through difficult things in life. Do not fall into toxic positivity. You want to feel what you feel, but not get stuck there. Gratitude may be a way to pull yourself out.

Fuel For Gratitude

If you want to have a happy life, then you should fuel it with happiness. Everyone wants to feel happy. The big question is: How can we be happy? Is it possible to be happy without consuming happiness?

The key is gratitude fuel. This includes all and any thing you can do that will help you appreciate even the smallest details of life. No matter how unhappy your life may be, happiness will fuel you. You must find ways to be grateful for everything you can.

The amount of gratitude fuel that you use should exceed all the negative aspects about your life. This means that, the more you feel miserable about your life, the more gratitude you must give yourself every day.

Find Gratitude in the midst of a rough life

Everyday you meet people with great lives and then there are those whose lives could be improved. People who are looking for a better life share one thing in common. They lack the ability to be grateful for the things they have. They can't have more if they don't appreciate what they have. They don't have gratitude and can't get more.

There are always things you can be thankful for, regardless of how awful someone's lives might be. This realization and gratitude will lead to a positive change in their life.

If you complain you are focusing on what you believe are the problems. If the Universe sees there are no problems, then it will be able to help you. It is your responsibility to understand that everything was created by you and for yourself. You have the power to change the outcome of any situation you create, whether it be for the good or bad.

If you wish to lose everything in life, if life would be more difficult for you, if life would be less easy, if life would be hard, if life would be miserable, if life would make you feel unhappy, and you would love to have no one to love you.

You don't need to be happy if your life would be better.

Being grateful is a way to create abundance. Anxiety can cause poverty.

Stop being impressed with the world around you, and everything that is wrong in you life. You have the power to change how you see your life. Visualize your life as though it were already here. Your life will improve in all areas. As you feel more alive and joyful, the universe will make your life beautiful.

Your energy is already available to you. It doesn't matter how your life is, you control the power that can make it better. This knowledge should help you to be thankful for all the good things in your life and to appreciate all that is around you.

The gap between where your life is now and what you desire to be, whether it's physically, emotionally, relationally or financially, can feel very large.

Now is the time to put aside all your worries and focus on the things you are thankful for. This might mean you need to laugh about the things you value. You may find that many things are taken for granted.

If you want your life to change, if it is possible to use the law to attract things quicker, if this is something you desire, simply start to be grateful for what you already have. Gratitude can change your life. It is simple, fast, and powerful. It has the power to give you immediate results.

Take a moment to reflect on all the things in life that you are grateful for right now. You will be amazed at how many items you actually have. Being grateful for even the smallest of things can make your day a lot more enjoyable.

You must be grateful for everything you receive. It doesn't matter if you get a massage or a new car, happiness or inner peace, or a vacation, new job, money, love, or anything else.

Being grateful for all you want right now will tell the Universe that it is already yours and that you are open to taking it. This will increase your ability to manifest things faster by activating the law.

Consider yourself grateful for what you have attained right now. Allow your heart to overflow in gratitude. Each day, take the time and say "thanks." Before you leave your home each morning, you should repeat this 100 times. You can say it when you're in the shower. You can even say it while you're brushing your hair. You can also say it when getting dressed. Consider that each time you say "thanks," you are creating a powerful moment.

Throughout the day, say "thanks!" for every thing that happens. This will make you more open to the possibility of synchronicity. And you will find that you get more things than what you thought were possible.

Recall these things to increase your gratitude.

* We should be thankful that the sky is blue and clear.

* You should be thankful for the flowers blooming.

* Remember to be grateful for the comfy sheets you slept on last nights.

* I am grateful for the sweet old man who always smiles, and says hello.

* You should be grateful for the cuddles your pet gave you this morning.

* Take a moment to thank the cashier who gave your coupon.

* Give thanks for the roof above your head.

* Be grateful for what clothes you have.

* Enjoy your lunch break by taking a walk in the park.

* You should be grateful for your car everytime you drive it.

* Be grateful each morning that your body wakes up.

* Eat with gratitude every meal.

* Be thankful that you are able to see something in your favorite colors.

If all of this seems too overwhelming for you, consider creating a gratitude journal. This tool will help you believe that you can achieve your goals and set you up for success. It will also give you a positive outlook. A gratitude journal allows you to write down all that you are grateful. You must do this every single day.

Prior to going to bed every night, write down at most five to ten of the things that you are thankful for each night. You can keep your mind positive by writing down a list of gratitude every night before you go to bed. This helps you focus on all the good in your life. By focusing on your happiness, you can expect the best from your life. This helps you visualise your future in positive, meaningful ways.

A gratitude journal can help you look back on all of the things you are thankful for and to learn as much as you can. A gratitude journal allows you to reflect on the good aspects of yourself and your life that you wrote. This can boost your belief in yourself so that you can achieve your goals.

Growing your gratitude

At the end, just writing in a journal of gratitude may not help you cultivate the gratitude you desire or need. We recommend that you continue to write in the journal. However we will go over some additional ways to cultivate thankfulness so that you can raise vibrations whenever necessary.

1. Attention

It is important to notice your negative emotions, complain, or gossip. You should be aware of how you view the world. Are you angry when you see the car in front of you and start shouting at them? Are you going to let the circumstances of the day dictate your mood or are you able to breathe and be grateful? Then think about how grateful you are that this car is there to get you where I need it to.

2. You can change your point of view

After becoming more aware and keeping a gratitude notebook, change your outlook from negative or angry to grateful. This will take some time and lots of practice. You are responsible only for how you think. You can show gratitude by simply feeling that way.

3. Be a Quality-oriented person and not a Quantity-oriented one

Requiring someone to be grateful is not a good idea. This will lead to power imbalances which will ultimately undermine gratitude. Inauthentic expressions can result in gratitude feeling unauthentic. The key to fostering gratitude is creating spaces and times that allow for spontaneous expressions. Studies have repeatedly shown that gratitude fatigue is possible when you try to be grateful every day.

How can authenticity be conveyed? Details. Specificity is a way to increase appreciation. It shows someone that you are attentive and not just going through the motions.

4. Be humble

Humility can be defined as the "act of being modesty or respectful." Take stock of what you already take for granted and think about how you can change that attitude. Humility will encourage you to open yourself to new ways and transform your view of the world.

5. Share Appreciation

It's okay if you compliment someone. Let others know how grateful you are for what they bring to your life. Practice random acts de kindness and expect nothing in exchange. You can spread positivity and positive energy simply by being yourself.

6. Take a look at the Silver Lining

Make lemonade of your lemons. If you find yourself in a difficult circumstance, ask "what can we learn from it?" "How can we make sure this doesn't happen again?"

This is particularly useful for work, where it can make you more productive and move you away from a situation of loss. It is possible to turn obstacles into opportunities. In every situation there will be an opening.

7. Donate

Give of your energy, time and financial resources only when it is possible. If you're grateful for what your life has given you, join a cause close to you. Donating gives you the opportunity to live gratefully because it helps people and causes you care deeply about, and others who are less fortunate.

Trust that the Universe will provide for your needs.

Chapter 12: Profile Of Vibration

Your whole being, from the tissue in your heartbeat to the tips on your fingernails, emits a certain vibration. Matter is the vibrational status of energy. Recomposed energy can become force and material. Force can move matter. And matter can carry force. The water can move the ice, and you can see it floating in the water. Both can be moved by the water, and both can vibrate at different frequencies.

A fabric exists beneath space and the time, connecting all animate and inanimate objects. This fabric can be thought of as a link between people, thoughts and planets. Science has now confirmed the existence of this fabric, something ancient meditation teachers knew all along. They are called fields in scientific parlance. Every fundamental particle has its field. A vibration in such a field will give rise to the building blocks that make up matter. The

Large Hadron Collider is being tested in Switzerland. It's not for the purpose of finding particles. They have had a tremendous success.

It must now be obvious that you are an object which is vibrating constantly. Like a tuning tok. This field that vibrates to make us feel connected makes us all part of this universe. You are as connected with your twin as you would be to the Himalayan rock salt.

This connection to everyone and the vibrational profile, which makes you, and all other things, what they are everywhere, is how Law of Attraction operates.

Your vibration determines everything that you do. It is also the basis of who you are as you walk from cradle on to grave. It is not autonomous. It needs direction from you. Imagine a car heading down a hill. It will continue, regardless of your opinion. It will make it to the bottom. You can take control of your car and dictate its direction. Your life will bring you all kinds of things without you even knowing it. This power can be controlled by you.

Whatever you do, vibrate at a specific frequency. But there are ways you can influence that frequency. Vibration can be controlled through exercise. Meditation is another. Another way to raise your vibration is to exercise, dance, and listen to techno music. Meditation, rest, and classical music (think Bach or Vivaldi), will lower you vibration. Walking is an excellent way to control your vibration. The vibration you have been born with will be the vibration you experience. However, it is possible to change this vibration by using any of the methods described. Each person needs to determine the best way of controlling their vibration. The best way to identify the activity that will help you control your vibration is by looking at your body type.

How to find your Vibration Profile

There are three types general vibrational bodies. The person who is unable to gain weight no mater what they eat. These people are very energetic and well-trained. You can control your vibration by learning mindful meditation. Tune it down.

If you are a large, chubby individual who cannot lose weight or have oily complexion no matter how hard you try, it is best to perform intense exercises at least once daily followed by deep breath exercises. Your vibrational profile should be raised.

For the third body type you are the one who is neither the first two. For your vibration to rise, you should eat frequently and whenever you feel hungry. Regular exercise and regular meditation will get you to the frequency you desire and help you control your vibration. Avoid caffeine. For this type of body, you must be able manage the vibration swings without it getting too high/low.

Meditation can be used regardless of your body type. In order to achieve the highest vibrational frequency, it is important to use meditation, mindfulness, and reflection.

There are many methods of achieving optimal vibration. They all work on the same principle. Different body types have different vibrational levels. The higher the vibration, people are more active and tend to have higher metabolisms. People with low energy have slower metabolisms which makes them a little heavier.

Once you are clear about your body type and your vibration, you can start working towards your goal of finding your best vibration. If yoga is your thing, this will work in your favor.

Meditation and mindfulness are effective for all body types. There are meditation strategies you can use to raise your vibration. Your optimal vibration can only be achieved when you are at peace. Meditation automatically induces peace by raising or lowering energy levels without the practitioner even trying to figure out what they need to do to achieve that state.

Remember, it's all in the vibration. If you can get into the habit of striking the right frequency of sound, you will naturally be able to invoke the Law of Attraction.

Attuning To the Vibration of the Universe

You must tune in to the vibrations around you to make the LOA work. It increases your body's physical charge. This amplifies what you communicate verbally and mentally. Raising your vibration refers to how you feel. Being happy is the purpose of life. Therefore, you need to make sure that you are happy. There are many ways you can look at it.

You feel happier when you're in good mood. A positive mood is the ideal state in your life. You will find that your environment is more positive when you are happy and in good spirits. It's not easy to stay positive, so it's important that we work hard at it.

Being in a positive state of mind is a way to raise your vibration. You probably already know what motivates you to be in a good place. It could be listening to good music, exercising, meditating or going for a stroll. Although there are many options for optimizing your LOA, some are better than others. Dancing is hands-down the best way raise your vibration.

The combination of good music and exercise can allow you to relax your body and help you to connect with your mind. Through physical activity, the mind and body become one. You can experience an emotional rich and unthinkable state. The same as a runner's high.

Enjoy the time you have to drive and listen to the music that brings you joy. Dancing is one of those activities that you might enjoy more if the end result you are pursuing is already in your hands. This state of being can be used to make affirmations mentally, or even louder.

Consider Native Americans dancing around a campfire and chanting. They are creating a charge for energy that allows them to tap into their potential energy to get more done. Another example is that of the Turkey's Whirling Dervishes. They are a unique dancing style that places its practitioners in a high state of awareness.

Martial arts practicers may notice that many styles are based around a yin/yang idea. Body movements that flow smoothly into each other in rhythmic ways, almost as if they were dancing, is this not surprising? Traditional martial arts are built on the natural movements and rhythms of the body. It is because of this that some martial arts masters can move so fast and have such small movements as Bruce Lee's one inch punch. He was an expert in body mechanics, and he mentally merged with the flow.

Points to Consider

Setting goals is essential to reaching your goals. Consider all options and details to make your goal a fulfilling one. It is best to set a realistic goal if your LOA journey is just beginning. Once the target is achieved, you can always aim for higher. You should visualize your major goal, meditate daily, and be focused on it.

The minor goals flow from the major goal, and they become the steps to be taken to make that goal a reality. Do everything you can each day to make "the ending" possible.

Daily meditation, or simply taking the time to be present for the end result every day is essential. It's easy to lose sight of your goal and not care enough about achieving that goal. It's OK if this is true. You need to find a goal, which excites you and has deeper meaning for you.

For your dream to become a reality, it is important to do something every single day. It's worth making time for a 15 minute daily meditation. If this takes you too long, you aren't recognizing the value of focus or the power your subconscious mind wields over your conscious consciousness. Taking time for focus is like recalibrating the weapon that guides your eyes towards the target.

Spending time with you helps you realize your true goals in life. Only time can show you what it means to human beings, and make you more approachable and sympathetic to others. Understanding how other's minds work can offer insight into your own.

The best way to raise your vibration is to do it alone. Moving, exercising, listening, dancing and even taking long walks can bring you deeper insight. It is possible to raise your vibration through visualizations and affirmations.

You can create a new and better life by making a commitment to feeling and thinking differently. All you have is your past thoughts. A new future requires you to think and be constantly positive about the changes you desire, no matter what the environment is. Be visionary.

Exercise 1:

Write down five things that can help you grow your business. You can start by asking the questions below.

Can you join networks?

Is it possible to reach out, and learn from your peers, about what they have done to grow their businesses?

Do you have an online presence?

What should you do to improve your website?

Do you need an update for your office?

Can you learn a different skill?

Are you in need of a job?

Do you know what to do?

Make a detailed list and be sure to follow through.

Exercise 2:

Keep practicing each style of meditation. Then, you can stick with the one that is most soothing to your soul. It is best to meditate at night, before bed.

A good time to monitor your thoughts is after you've fully awakened. You might need more mental power to learn to remove yourself from your thoughts.

Exercise 3:

Refocus your eyes on your vision for five minutes each day.

Take control of the negative environment that controls your mind. You can use your emotions to guide you.

Exercise 4:

Spend some time doing things you enjoy. It is important to find activities that will make you feel as though you are living the "end", and to show gratitude for your efforts.

Chapter 13: Love Unconditionally

It's important to recognize that love doesn't involve blaming others. Each and everyone of us are unique. It is this uniqueness that gives us our place among the universe. That's our purpose. We want our individuality and want to be different. Why do we get upset when others are different from us? They are two sides of one coin. Respect your differences, and love the other person just as much as you love you. The more you can see this, you'll discover your true nature. It is a powerful feeling. It's like the wave which looks at the calm, distinguishing it from it as the stronger until it realizes they are both one thing: water. The Universe is powerful when you are open to accepting everyone, no matter their differences. I will also show how to see the beauty in every situation and how you can turn a misstep into a step.

To give love is to be forgiven. Giving love can help you forgive, while forgiving will allow you to remain in the now. It gives power to the present.

Power of Now

The power and ability to live in the now is a simple concept. However, it can be confusing and difficult to practice and understand because of the constant stream distractions and misinterpretations of its nature. The power that now isn't a physical force we have, it's a mental strength. But it manifests in the world. The power and ability to live in the now is not dependent on your mental structure. The power and ability to live in the moment is all about staying focused. Practice the power to now in order to magnify your vibration so you attract your opportunities to manifest what you want.

The common argument against keeping the current moment is that it blinds the mind to the consequences we are taking, exposes us and hinders our ability to build a better future. These are only true when we waste the moments we have. It is enough to build in the moment that we have, and all that will happen in the future moments.

Forgiveness is key to the power and potential of the moment. This is because it is one the attributes that ishes away any conduit linking past transgressions to today. After all is forgotten, forgiveness is the key to making the next moment fresh.

Peace is a feeling that can attract the power to now. This peace is available in many places, and you can find it in many ways. You could increase your joy by being with your loved one, taking care or pets, or even doing charitable acts. If you find joy in everything you do, you can attract the power now. Giving love and seeking forgiveness can bring you inner peace and help you manifest your desires more effectively.

One common misconception of fear is that we should eliminate it entirely. It may sound like a good idea, but fear serves a purpose. Instead of suppressing fear, respond to fear with faith. Fear is like the messenger who brings bad news. If you kill the messenger, bad tidings can never go away.

There are two sides to the physical world. The brain and the body. The element called consciousness is contained within the brain. The body does not refer to just the organs and space that we use. It also encompasses all important things that help preserve the body. The brain is responsible for all of this. There is also the mind built on top of it, which we will discuss later. The consciousness, which we will examine as we navigate the landscape of this book, is also important.

Brain and mind are connected to bring together the phenomenal aspect of the universe and the noumenal part of our existence. It becomes difficult when explaining the concept of focus and observation in a realistic way. Most explanations only provide a general overview and are of little use. We are here to expose the truth.

The best way to see the root causes of adult problems is by looking at children's behavior. It is through deep observation that you can discover the secrets to living peacefully. It is essentially the power of now that holds the key to this secret.

This is the most powerful characteristic of a child, and it's what we lose during the transitory phase of puberty. This is mostly due to external influences. It's often thought that the loss is due to the loss or innocence. But, it's just part of being human. Then, we assume that we simply have to live with it. It is a long, tortuous path of false observations and consequences that leads to millions of people in discord, depression, and a living hell.

The Present

If there is one thing that you want to learn, and what you want for your children to learn, it is to embrace now. There are challenges, but you can do it by digging into the moment. Most are found at the cellular level. Because we get bored of the present, we tend to want to leave it. We don't seem understand that each moment is a separate nondimensional piece of that time and space. There is much more. What we can do is to look at it in wonder to see even more than what our first glance shows. The present is not dull. The present is not good or evil, happy nor sad. The present moment, while not a consequence, is an independent event. You should respect it without worry, malice and prejudice.

It is common to argue against the idea of living in the present moment. This blinds us and exposes us and others to dangers that may be beyond our control.

If you are able to see the possibilities and control them, you will be able to accept the facts in this rebuttal. It also assumes your initiating actions will be less than ideal and that allies outnumber foes. It's even worse if you believe that you must look to the future in order to live a better and more fulfilling life. No. The present must be improved in order to build a better world.

Because of the freedom you have to use this moment to your advantage, it is a powerful moment in time. You can't change the past. And you can't make the future. But, you can, and will, influence the moment. You have less time to spend on the current if you invest resources in the future.

A Child's innocence

What is the child's reaction to stressful situations? It could be that he fell, or that he was disciplined at home by a parent. They respond in their own way. They might cry or feel sad. However, within a matter of minutes, they are right as water. Everything seems to flow as effortlessly as a hand on time. There's no need to hold back or harbor animosity. All that is required is for you to forgive the actor/actress. Perfect. Now they can just move on to their new moment and take it all in. There are no expectations when they arrive at the next moment. This is because he was not thinking about the new one in the previous moment. Therefore, disappointments are not possible when there are no expectations. The other thing to remember is that if the moment you are experiencing is identical to the one you were expecting, acceptance will prevail over joy.

It's a first experience with icecream. I vividly recall my child's first encounter with icecream. His first experience with ice cream was a pure joy. It spread to everyone around him. It's powerful because it builds you up and allows you to fight off any challenges.

Contrary to having something positive happen in every moment of time, there is also the possibility of something not so great. This can take place in one of two ways. If something isn't so good, you may be surprised to find that the entire time prior is filled in with joy and peace. If you fear something will happen in the near future, you are more likely to live in a worse place than it is. FDR once said, "Nothing can be feared except fear itself."

Consider the example above. The child fell and then forgot about the incident, moving on. Instead of not expecting it, imagine if the child worried that he would fall. That fear would cause great distress and probably prevent him from walking. You can't live your whole life like that. Fear should not be banished, but instead you should live in this moment. Fear is a safety feature, not a retardant.

Living in each moment is the greatest power anyone can develop. This power is what we were born with, but it soon becomes a loss to fear and memory.

This book will show us the steps we need to take to live in the present moment. Without having laid the base, it is impossible to view the top of the pyramid. Everything else is just a projection of this moment. You must be here right now. Here, in this space, you can make the rest of life as wonderful as possible.

Looking at the power to now from the point of manifestation, you'll see that the path to effortless manifestation lies in your ability to forgive others, give love and remain present. These are all things we were taught as kids, but something happened to make it difficult to remember them.

Chapter 14: Practical Techniques In Healing The Mind

Self-healing & psychosomatic diseases

And yet, not many people can actually practice self-healing skills despite all the hype.

Before we begin to answer the question about how to heal your mind with your mind, let's examine the origin of the physical problem: the disease, the pathology or the accidental event.

My view, which has been shared more and more in medical-scientific environments is that almost all of the diseases we suffer from have an "psychosomatic" component or an origin.

If our mind is in stress, and we feel fatigue, tension, or restlessness then our mind won't be able activate our defenses against external agents. This leaves us more vulnerable to attack.

Personally, I believe that accidents such as a vehicle accident or a falling object, injuries, are connected to unconscious motivations. They have exposed us and led to the trauma.

In other words, the most advanced theories of Mental Dynamics to which the Sailfulness Method refers, claim that the connections mind-body-events-disease-healing can be set in a harmonious way, greatly increasing the duration and especially the quality of life of individuals. You can also expose them to less risk, even accidental.

In cases of imbalance, the mind may even be able to trigger the illness, thus making us "safe", from a stressful situation.

You can think of people who go into work each day feeling stressed by their bosses. It activates an unconscious mechanism in these cases that reduces your defenses.

People are "physically sick". The flu and fever can then be treated.

Our bodies produce, via various glands substances, that have active ingredients very similar or many medicines we take. At the same time, our bodies can also concentrate toxic and tensions with effects very similar or identical to the diseases that effect us.

The Placebo Effect

You cannot talk about self healing and healing with your mind without briefly illustrating the Placebo Effect in conjunction with Mental Dynamics techniques.

Studies have shown that patients who are given fake treatments such as sugar and water to act as an anti-inflammatory, or even a surgery can heal very well. Why is this so?

Most people believe that pseudo-care induces positive beliefs that affect the body's physiology.

However, scholars are beginning to call it the "Nocebo Effect", but we believe that the reverse is also true.

Negative beliefs can lead to negative physiological effects. This can make it difficult for us to use our natural self-healing tools.

This concept is best understood with an example. Some social conventions have a tendency to respond automatically to the trivial query "how are your friends?" "It's fine", "let's get on with things", and "it's not too bad." Some cultures are conservative and prudent, such as the one from Italy.

One important point: Pay attention to the word "not bad". Negations can fool the mind, as they are abstracted concepts. Instead, the mind focuses on the word evil with all its negative connotations.

It is important to avoid double negations in mental dynamics and transform "there are no evils" into "good".

Recalling social conventions as a response to how you look, you might ask "How are your eyes?" You can ask the same question in Los Angeles, but not in Manchester. You'll find that Americans tend to say "good" while British people will answer "not very bad". "Give us five!" Brilliant! ".

We should not be surprised that Americans have achieved a dominating position in the global economy through their positive mental attitude.

The placebo effect exists. It is scientifically supported. Each student will be able to activate it with a positive mental attitude.

Autoscopy

Our body is made up many interconnected systems. Bone system. Muscle system.

Nervous System. Organs. Lymphatic System. Cardiovascular System.

We have created powerful tools that enable us to study the anatomy of each system and organ. You can use X-rays or MRI scans as well as ultrasound and CT scans.

What if we could use the powerful placebo contribution to our physical well being to make our minds a scanner that detects tensions and contracts?

Take control of your mind

Science medicine, as we know and understand it today, is a relatively recent development in human history.

For millennia, people relied on healers. Shamans, sorcerers, and shamans. Their solutions were often only partially related to active principles.

While I can't deny the important of modern medical research, it would not be wise to replace chemotherapy treatment with an appeal to the spirits the ancestors. The fundamental importance of the mind for self-healing process would be extremely limited if we didn't consider it.

Curing the mind can be done, although it cannot replace official medicine.

Self-healing is also an option to manage pain. This is not only about healing with the mind but also living better in difficult or sick conditions.

Modern medicine, ancient and modern

All ancient medicine relies on self-healing.

Natural methods of health are being discovered more often than ever, in particular at the moment.

The allopathic approach which treats the symptoms of the disease rather than its cause has been abandoned in favor of a more responsible approach.

New (holistic) vision regards man as the inseparable whole body, mind, spirit. Here, it is recognized that the true cause of disease is inside oneself.

This knowledge has been a basis of ancient medicine. However, "official" medicine has long taken this into account. PNEI studies the interplay between the immune, nervous system, and psyche. This confirms the close link between thoughts/emotions with our health.

How to promote self - healing

Although self-healing is an instinctive and natural process, there are times when a condition that causes a significant imbalance in the body. This could make it impossible to heal or even difficult.

A few good practices and techniques can be applied to ensure that our system is in the best possible condition. These are just some.

Nutrition

It is essential to maintain good health. The body's health is dependent on nutrition. Studies have shown that maintaining an alkaline body is closely connected to good health.

Veganism and vegetarianism have enormous health benefits.

You can also count on food supplements or superfoods to boost your energy levels and maintain good health.

Rest

The brain clears out toxins and helps to restore balance during sleep. A good night's rest is crucial to keep the body healthy and relieve stress. A state of congestion is when the body cannot perform its functions correctly because it is under too much stress.

It is vital to get 8 hours of sleep a night or more, depending on your body's needs.

Thoughts, emotions

Also, our thoughts as well as emotions must be taken into account. We all know that many diseases are psychosomatic. This means that our mental and emotional health can be negatively affected.

Expressing one's emotions and controlling one's thought patterns can help to improve health and promote self-healing.

Realizing the power in our minds, we discover that thoughts, words and sentences can have a profound effect on the health of our cells, as well as the DNA.

Techniques, disciplines

Many holistic practices and some spiritual practices are available to us for our good health and healing. Here are some:

Meditation - Studies that have examined meditation have shown that it can reduce stress and anxiety, improve mental clarity, stimulate vital energy, and speed up healing.

Reiki, Theta Healing - Some techniques, such as Reiki and Theta Heating allow us to rebalance energies and to deeply address mental patterns or energy blocks.

Yoga, Tibetan Rites - Yoga is an ancient science that can help restore harmony between body and mind.

Reflexology, Acupuncture. These are ancient Chinese medical practices that, when combined with a preventive approach allow the body's health to be maintained.

Bach Flowers, Essential Oils — Naturalopathy can have subtle but profound effects on the health of the mind and body. This is especially true when essential oils are used in combination with massage techniques.

Music Therapy — The use of specific sound frequencies such as music at 432, mantras or sound therapy to promote harmony within the body and mind.

Many people across the globe have witnessed miraculous healings without drugs or medical protocol.

A new vision for health allows even the most severe diseases to be treated.

Healing = Self-healing

It would suffice to comprehend that all that happens is our fault, and to know that we can make it better.

The role of each individual in healing is crucial. We can also say that healing always depends on self-healing.

No matter the type or amount of healing activity used, the basic principle is the body's inherent ability of restoring balance and health.

Chapter 15: Believing You Cannot

Fear is the strongest emotion of all that can affect your chances of attracting what you want. Did you ever feel stressed or anxious about how your life might turn out? If you answered yes, you're not the only one. You must devise a strategy to change these thoughts. Fear will limit your potential and make it difficult to achieve your goals. However, fear will only hold you back. Instead of being focused on your fears and limiting thoughts of what is possible, love will lift you up and fill you with positivity. We'll be looking at some methods to get rid of those fears so you can believe in yourself and turn them into love.

To radiate your love

It is admirable to want to transform the world with love. You must first learn how change yourself and your relationships. This is done by raising the vibration of your love and radiating it as much as you can.

Love can be radiated by humans if they are open to love for themselves and others.

Light travels through space, becomes entangled in a gravity field, and then attracts material. This attraction then turns into through. The information is what talks to our bodies and guides us to act and think and feel or speak. When it's channeled through your heart, light energy becomes the power of human beings to make their goals a reality. People who love are able to emit vibrations at an extremely high frequency. A person who is not in love with another person will emit vibrations that are lower frequency. The law if love says that the energy we send out will attract more.

Let's consider it from the standpoint of building healthy, loving relationships. Relationships are not the only reason you should send love. However, it's the easiest way to see.

Let's say you had some terrible experiences growing up in relation to the idea and concept of love. It could be you were cheated or sexually abused. You can't control everything that happens to your life, even though like attracts like. There will be times when you are the victim of circumstance. It is the fault of the other person.

If you've ever been through something like this, it is likely you will experience many of the same painful emotions. You might feel physically shaking, crying or experience the same pain over and over.

These "love stories" will affect how you approach loving relationships. You may have been hurt previously, so it is important to ensure that you don't get hurt again. This will cause you to become closed-off. It is dangerous to be vulnerable if you are afraid of being open. This causes you to be resistant to the idea of letting someone else in.

Fear is the root cause of this problem. Fear of being hurt is what drives you to take measures to protect your self. Fear causes you to retreat from the world and avoid taking any actions. It will make you resentful of love. Living in fear will prevent you from allowing love in. Let go of your past fears, and any emotions they have connected to them. That is the only way to allow love to enter your life. If you hold on to the past, the more you repel love.

Your highest level of soul potential is reached when you can love others. This can lead to a higher level of performance in all areas, including creativity and health, as well a more positive effect on the environment. This is the time for you to see that you are a change agent. Your vibration must be raised to spread love and joy throughout the world.

If more people used the energy of love to transform their negative emotions and thoughts into positive ones, it would make the world the most powerful transformational force ever. When our hearts are open to positive emotions and thoughts we naturally emit an electromagnetic field that can positively affect the surrounding environment and all living things.

Your life can be transformed by changing your thoughts, your words, your actions and your behavior. This knowledge can help to see yourself and your power as a source of energy. You are able and able to listen, rather than follow the belief systems, ideas, or direction of others.

Be Free from Your Fears

It is important to understand how to deal with your fears in order to find the love you desire. This will require that you analyze your worries and pinpoint the root cause of your unhappiness. This is not an easy task. It can also be frightening for some. Fears are often ignored because people fear that they may find something they don't like. If you want your emotions to grow and you want to manifest the life you dream of, then you must confront them instead of hiding.

1. Embody and Master

It is crucial to remember that fear does not have to be suppressed or denied. This skill is extremely useful. It's important that you can fully accept the emotions you feel, then acknowledge them, and then find ways to process them so you can let them go. It is possible to express your feelings through creative activities, such music, painting or writing.

2. Fears must be let go

Although this may seem counterintuitive, it will allow you to be more aware of your fears. This will help you deal with your issues and make a decision. You must be willing to take the time to write down your problems. Doing so can help you see that not all of your fears are true. This will make it easier to forget your fears.

However, you may find yourself with fears that aren't there. This is a good thing. Most people have fears. We have subconsciously hidden them for so long, that they don't realize that they still exist. Knowing your hidden fears is a positive thing. You can then process them.

3. Demystify Fears

Fears are almost always unknowable. For instance, think back to those times when you felt the creeping unease, a heavy heartbeat, or fear that you might fail. But you don't fully understand what you are feeling or why. It is important to try to understand fear in order to make more space for love. Face it straight away and work out how to deal with it. Most likely, you'll find your limiting beliefs and how they are holding you back. In order to change those negative beliefs, you will need to start using affirmations and a wheel.

Replacing Your Fears

Once you have faced your fears honestly and decided they are not a secret anymore, you will be able to move forward with getting rid of them. You've taken the most important first step. You are aware of what you fear, and now have the power to change that. Let's talk about some ways we can help you approach fear in a totally different way.

1. Do Good

At the end we all desire to be heard, appreciated, and seen by others. The best thing you can do is sit down with someone and offer an open ear, regardless of their opinions. Be there for them, show empathy, and help them to understand. This type and amount of love will make a significant difference in the lives of your other loved one. It will also help you feel more compassionate. If you begin to feel anxious, think about what you could do to show love that way.

2. Connect a special object to your transformation

A specific object may be something you've connected to your law o of attraction goal. Why not connect it with fear and love? You can use a small stone to do this because it is easy to hold in your hand. You can imagine fear pouring in to the rock and then love spreading through your body. An alternative idea is to add a piece or jewelry that you can keep on your person all day as a reminder of love and focus. You can also pick a candle with a relaxing scent.

3. Stay open

Even though you might be open-minded, it is normal to shut down when you experience fear. Keep your mind open to all possibilities and fight against fear whenever it starts to affect you. Consider what you could do differently to feel better. Start by asking yourself how you could improve the situation. Next, make small but significant changes that will allow you to step out of your comfort zones. Finally, ask others for their help when needed. Don't conceal your worries. Use the support system you've created to help you feel secure and confident.

4. Share your love

It is possible to share your love by showing understanding and compassion to others. There are other methods to share love. Meditations that focus on heart imagery can help you send love out to others. This could be for someone in need, someone who is in bad shape, or just to wish them well. This little act can help bring you into harmony with abundance. It will also put you in a better position to manifest all you want.

Additionally, you could also try the random act or kindness that you do each day.

Doubting the Law of Attraction

This is where most people experience fear or doubt. They are concerned about whether or not the law is working for their benefit. This causes resistance. This is normal. Once you recognize that these are present, you can work with your team to get rid of them.

There is a good possibility that the steps you've just completed will relieve some anxiety and help you feel like you're on the right track. There are some things you can do that will help with fear of manifesting. You need to get out from the realm of fear. You don't need to worry whether or not the law os attraction works. You need to trust that the law is working and it is unfolding as it should.

It is important to realize that you have the ability to change. If you are experiencing fear or worry, you most likely have a unresolved issue. It is possible to change this problem. It is possible for you to make changes. It doesn't matter what you do, as long as you are willing and able to change.

It is possible to start getting rid of fear if you take the time necessary to discover where your fear stems from. You will eventually notice a change in the way things are. You aren't worried or afraid. You start to feel at ease and can face any worries with calm.

Do not let your fantasy of love look different than it actually is. Oprah said it best: "When love isn't wrapped up in our personal fantasies, we fail to recognize that it exists."

Chapter 16: Building Your Vision For Abundance

Chapter 3 dealt with being clear about the things you want to see in the universe. This chapter will assist you in getting the universe to manifest abundance in life. We will discuss ways to revive your imagination and let go of foolish beliefs that you once held dearly as children.

Do you remember being a kid and believing that sheets draped across a washing-line were a castle? The trusted family dog was a dangerous snake and the trusted pet dog was a dangerous dragon? Or that a broomstick, a noble steed, was a noble horse. Prince and Princess enjoyed a royal feast of mudpies on a pile full of leaves. Our imaginations were capable of taking us to exotic places, where anything was possible.

We were content, happy and fulfilled with all of the hopes and dreams that we had.

This age of innocence was lost somewhere in our adolescent days. Instead of being filled by hope and anticipation, we began accepting other limiting beliefs. These limiting beliefs became part of our subconscious and made us fearful and doubtful about everything. While it is fine to have an open mind and to ask questions, the problem for most of us was that these limiting beliefs and doubts impeded our creativity and prevented us from feeling the joy, happiness and contentment that the universe thrives upon.

I want you to feel confident that you can let your imagination go free by the end.

"Your subconscious will work tirelessly with your brain to achieve the affirmations and images of your goals," Jack Canfield. You are bound to succeed when your subconscious mind is filled with affirmations and images that reflect your goals.

Visualize what You Want

You've already discovered that the universe responds primarily to our emotions. Because of this, it is crucial that any visualization or technique we use be as precise as possible. You have already written down the goals in Chapter 3. Take a moment to look at the areas you have divided up your life into. Then, take a moment to consider the goals and the dates that you would like to see them realized.

You should choose five to ten goals to be achieved in each area of your life within the next six months. Vision boards in combination with written goals can be a powerful tool for encouraging the universe that we will achieve what we want. Both of these are extremely powerful and I have witnessed miracles and goals in my own life.

Because of the power and synergy of the two, I also want to share some words.

Be realistic with your goals. But, if you really feel the universe is listening, push the limits a bit. My vision board was made in December of last year. By June/July nearly all of what I had envisioned on my vision boards had been achieved. The universe is generally always willing to take on the challenge. Most people think that the simplest goals will be easiest to achieve. This is a mistake. The universe will deliver no matter how bizarre or absurd your goal is at the time.

Create A Vision Board

This is where the real fun begins! Use a piece if cardboard, large frames, or a digital program to make a visual representation and visualization of your hopes, dreams, goals, wishes, and desires for the next six- to twelve months. I prefer to mix up the goals, so I use a large board that spans the length my desk. It is important to remember that different things work for different people. The information I am sharing has been what I have found works well for me for the past ten years. Here are some of the mistakes that I made as I tried to attract what I wanted in my life with vision boards.

Let me just mention the negatives. In 2008, my business was quite successful and I had been using visionboards as a method of goal setting since 2008. I was experiencing some scary health issues, so much of the vision board was intended to be healed completely. Unfortunately, I had placed on the same visionboard a symbol which represented my company at that time. My business has grown exponentially over the past few years, expanding rapidly in a very short amount of time. The symbol was placed on its sides, representing defeat. It was this way that my business went bust before 2008. However, I learned a valuable lesson about the power that vision boards can have.

The following tips are for creating your visionboard: Be aware that the universe may give you contradictory or contradicting information. A good example would be to get a promotion at work that would require you to be away from your home every day. Instead, you would want to spend more of your time with your loved ones. Can you see the contradiction between these two objectives?

Don't be vague when you ask for something. The visual representation should be accompanied by a date, just as you did when you wrote out your goals. If your goal is tied to money give the exact amount, and the time. If you're looking to lose weight, indicate the target weight or dress size you would like to reach by... (specify the date).

Your vision board has power because of the images/pictures it contains. The internet allows you to search for images that will best represent your goals and you have access to thousands or thousands of them. You can even take photos of the real thing, which is even more powerful. This is particularly true if your goal is to find the perfect home, car you want, or other tangible experience. You can do this easily by going around the neighborhood and searching for houses you like. A few photos can be saved to your visionboard as powerful reminders that this is the place you want!

Arrange to test drive the new vehicle and have the salesman take a photo of the two of you, either standing behind it or with it. It is more than just seeing yourself in a photo of the car. It also gives you an idea of what it will be like to actually experience the car.

After you've found some inspiring images, photographs, and maybe even a few motivational quotes, it's now time to put them all together.

Use your imagination to arrange the images so they speak to and inspire you. Your vision board should be fun. It will encourage you to visualize what you want. You can stick the images down or use a clear cover to protect them. The last thing you want is for the images to become damaged or to fade or fall apart.

The final step in the process is to ensure that you have your visionboard somewhere that you can easily see every day. For me, I keep it on my desk near my heart and am reminded daily of what I set for myself.

Make sure to look at your vision board frequently and keep track of how many of you have achieved your goals and dreams. Sometimes these dreams are almost miraculous. When you see that you have achieved anywhere from 50 to 75% of your goals, it is time to begin working on the next.

This is what I have found to be the most effective, but you may find other methods that work well for you. Some people prefer a digital visionboard that functions as a screensaver, whether it's for their iPhone, tablet, or computer. This can also serve as a way to take your digital vision board with you wherever you go and keep a record of all the items on your wish list. A digital visionboard is a great way to keep track of your dreams and goals. You can even change your board if something stops resonating with or you realize you have contradicting goals.

Others prefer a pinboard for their images, photos, and sometimes notes. A pinboard is almost like a digital visionboard in real life. In addition to searching for appropriate images online and taking photographs that reflect what you want, you can also search magazines for images that will inspire, such as Pinterest. There are so many ways to find inspiration.

I'd like to close this chapter by saying that no matter what option you choose, allow your imagination to run wild and have lots of fun. Even if it isn't your forte, this is an opportunity to get creative. It's possible to be completely surprised by the results. It is important that you do this work for yourself. Your vision is unique and the universe is your wish list. You can't expect another person to understand your vision or write down your dreams. This is where the real work begins. You must feel what it will feel like to experience the feeling of having, being, or doing what you want. It's the vibration of feeling to which the universe responds. You can live a little and still have a lot of fun.

Chapter 17: Never Give Up

The first rule for success is to never give up, no mater what. Many times, we find ourselves in a difficult situation on the path to success and are tempted not to keep trying. The journey to success is not easy. It requires that you are prepared to fail.

Everyone feels despair and doubt when life gets difficult. No matter how lofty or small your goals, you will have to face difficult periods when your motivation and commitment will be tested. This is when self doubt creeps in and you feel hopeless. But remember, tough times are only temporary, they don't last. Quitting should never be an option when you have a purpose and a goal. If you believe in your pursuit deeply, you will persevere over any obstacles which might cause you to quit.

If you give in to the temptations of giving up, you will wonder for the rest in your life if it was worth the effort. It is essential that you have the will to endure the most difficult temptations and to persevere on the road to success if you want to succeed. It's a fact that if you quit, it is almost certain that you won't reach your goals.

Why you shouldn't give in to your own self-preservation

A money-success mindset is not something you can give up.

1. You are much more than the temptation that you want to quit.

Your purpose and goals will surpass the temptation of quitting. Your journey to success is worth the effort and hard work you've put in. You can overcome challenges. Believe in yourself. Remember that hard times will pass.

2. It's all about the mind.

Your mental outlook is crucial in deciding whether to quit fighting or not. Your mental strength and ability to deal with problems and overcome them is the key to success.

3. Success isn't an easy road.

Just to be clear: success does not come easy. To see the end, it takes perseverance and hardwork. Be ready to face whatever life throws at us.

4. Success does not come overnight

Successful is a slow and patient process. You cannot achieve success overnight. If you enter the path to success with the mindset of making it big in a day, you are much more likely than others to be disappointed. Many people think successful people can get there overnight.

However they'll tell you that success takes hard work and perseverance.

5. Quitting will be a habit.

Once you quit, you will have a history of half-done, halb achieved aspirations or goals. It is easy to turn failure into a pattern. As with all habits it is important to practice repetition.

How to keep going and stay motivated

To achieve and maintain your goals, you need to have focus and motivation. For you to remain motivated on your path to success, it is important to have unwavering devotion to reach the goals you set. There is no one-size fits all solution for achieving our purpose or vision. Instead, we need to keep working hard and stay focused to ensure that your goal becomes a reality. It is easier to accomplish your goals if you have focus.

These are some things that can help you keep your focus and motivate yourself to achieve your goals.

1. Negative thoughts can be kept away

Negative thoughts hinder the achievement of goals. Negative thoughts should be kept away and replaced with positive affirmations and thoughts about success. Negative thoughts can make it impossible to succeed at anything. Even in the face of failure, find the positive things and the small victories.

2. Failure is acceptable

Nobody expects to be successful all of the time. Accept that you may fail, and accept that failures are normal in pursuit of your goals. Do your best to reach your goals. If you fail to achieve your goal, don't lose heart. Instead, look at the accomplishments and consider how you can make the most of them for future success.

3. Accept that your success is your responsibility.

No excuses or finger-pointing--success or failure in the pursuit of your goals is your sole responsibility. Once you understand that you have the ability to make or break your achievement you will never stop believing in the importance of it and will work hard to ensure that your goals become a reality.

4. Do not try to be too hard on yourself.

In the pursuit of wealth, perfection is not an option. Keep your support system strong and push yourself to succeed. If you are not successful, it will be a distraction from your ability to focus and motivate yourself.

5. Forget about the Vergangenheit

Perhaps you didn't reach a milestone, or didn't meet the deadline. Don't let these setbacks hold you back from moving forward in confidence. It is okay to face difficulties. Get up and keep moving. Negative thinking and negative emotions can encourage bad feelings. It is important not to let the past dictate your future.

6. The possible is what you should be focusing on.

Don't let your ambitions or unrealistic goals distract you from your goal. You must focus on the possible. While focusing on the possible, remember to always evaluate your capabilities and positive qualities.

7. Being consistent.

To be consistent, you must be willing and able take the necessary steps to make your goals a reality. It's the ability to resist and overcome distractions in order to keep your eyes focused on the price. You must be consistent by repeating the same actions over and over until you become accustomed to them. This helps your brain to learn the routines that will help to accomplish your goals. If you practice a consistent behavior each day, your brain will find it easier to convert it into habit.

Learn from your Failures and Get Up

You should not view failure as a defeat and the end to our pursuits. Instead, look at it as an opportunity to grow and learn. Seek out the lessons you can take from your failures, and use them as a tool to increase your success and wealth. You will be able to learn from your failures and become stronger in the face of any future setbacks. You cannot fail if the quit button is pushed. Do not allow the fear of failing to discourage you from following your dreams.

You will never be successful. Your journey towards your goal will not be easy. You will meet many obstacles and hurdles. Mental preparation is essential to ensure that you aren't distracted from your goal or become overwhelmed. Whatever your goal may be, regardless of how big or small it is, you must know that you will encounter difficult hurdles, failures, and other obstacles along the way.

The difference between success or failure is how mentally strong you are to face and overcome any obstacles that may come up.

First, accept and acknowledge that there will always be obstacles. Be mentally ready to face any obstacle and move on to the next step. The key is to have the ability to face and overcome any roadblocks. You need to learn to overcome any obstacles that may come up as you strive to achieve your goals.

Here are some tips to help overcome any roadblocks in your quest for success:

1. Identify the possible obstacles.

Before you embark on your journey toward wealth creation, it is important to review your goals to determine what obstacles you might encounter. It is impossible not to see everything. If you are careful about examining the goals that you have set, you will be able to anticipate many obstacles.

We don't want people to think about all the possible roadblocks. However, effective goal setting planning involves identifying potential obstacles and outlining ways to overcome them. An action plan will include addressing the problems. It is a good idea to make a list ahead of any possible obstacles that may arise and to have a contingency plan in place for dealing with them. There are many obstacles that can arise, both externally and internally. External ones include lack of money and internal ones like fear and self doubt.

2. Recognize and accept the 'false Hope Syndrome.

False hopes syndrome is a condition that involves setting a goal, then being disappointed by how hard it takes, and then giving up. False hopes are when people believe they will get quick results but then find out that this is not true. Setting goals is not a time to get excited. Keep in mind that goals can take time. Be realistic. Set clear, achievable mini-goals. It can be helpful to set small goals and celebrate your successes in order to keep your momentum up.

3. Accept challenges as learning opportunities.

People who see difficulties as an opportunity to grow are more likely be positive about their ability and potential success. Do not let your failures get you down, instead learn from them and focus on the positive. While it is true that successful people face less setbacks than those who give in, the difference is how they view obstacles.

4. Don't try to be perfect.

You can become distracted and lose your focus by being obsessed with perfection. You won't feel like you can achieve your goals if you hold yourself to unrealistic standards. Do not put too much pressure on yourself. Be kind to yourself and realize that mistakes and challenges can happen.

Positive thinking is an effective way to help people adapt and learn. Instead focusing on negative aspects of their mistakes, instead remind yourself that every setback can be a learning experience, regardless of how horrible.

5. Stay passionate.

Simply put, stay passionate. You can keep your passion and drive alive to help you focus on your goals. Be clear about what you want to achieve, even if you face difficulties.

6. Revise your goals.

Sometimes all you need to stay focused and on target is a revision or two of your goals. Your goals may need to be revised to keep your interest and to give you new ideas, plans, or even to get rid of them altogether.

Attitude is the key to maintaining focus. With the right attitude you can maintain your mental focus, increase your success chances and stay focused on the goal setting process. You have to know how to influence and nurture the right mindset within yourself in order to remain focused and motivated.

To achieve and pursue your goals, you must keep your focus. For you to remain focused through the goal-setting process, it is important to have the determination and motivation to succeed at your goal. Since there is no easy way to accomplish our purpose or vision, it takes dedication and perseverance to see your goal become a reality. Focusing on your goals will help you manifest them so it is easier to achieve.

While they are difficult to maintain, motivation and focus are vital to achieve your goals. These tips and others will help you remember the importance and motivate you to reach your goals.

You must accept setbacks as part of any endeavor. Roadblocks need not stop you from achieving your goals. Analyze the circumstances that are causing you to face a setback. If you can manage it, do it. Otherwise, look for a way to work around it.

Keep your eyes open and keep your focus. As you've probably heard, not all things go according to plan. For those who are determined to succeed, it is important to remember your past successes and not give up. To be more successful, you should overcome any setbacks. Never stop trying.

Conclusion

Next is to begin using the knowledge, guided meditations and hypnosis on daily basis. The best way to get the best results is to practice it regularly. You can also choose to use affirmations. These affirmations are great to repeat throughout the day, whenever you need to remind yourself how powerful you really are and what goals are important for you. All that matters is that you align your vibrations with what you desire. Don't let negative thoughts or events in your world bring you down.

Everything you've learned and everything you've read in this book, put it to work. Remember, knowledge without action will get you nowhere.

www.ingramcontent.com/pod-product-compliance
Lightning Source LLC
Chambersburg PA
CBHW050406120526
44590CB00015B/1842